chickamauga 1863

the river of death

JAMES ARNOLD

chickamauga 1863

the river of death

Praeger Illustrated Military History Series

PRAEGER

Westport, Connecticut
London

Library of Congress Cataloging-in-Publication Data

Arnold, James R.
    Chickamauga 1863: the river of death / James R. Arnold.
      p. cm. – (Praeger illustrated military history, ISSN 1547-206X)
    Originally published: Oxford: Osprey, 1992.
    Includes bibliographical references and index.
    ISBN 0-275-98440-0 (alk. paper)
    1. Chickamauga, Battle of, Ga., 1863. I. Title. II. Series.
    E475.81.A85   2004
    973.7'34–dc22   2004049506

British Library Cataloguing in Publication Data is available.

First published in paperback in 1992 by Osprey Publishing Limited, Elms Court,
Chapel Way, Botley, Oxford OX2 9LP. All rights reserved.

Copyright © 2004 by Osprey Publishing Limited

Library of Congress Catalog Card Number: 2004049506
ISBN: 0-275-98440-0
ISSN: 1547-206X

Praeger Publishers, 88 Post Road West, Westport, CT 06881
An imprint of Greenwood Publishing Group, Inc.
www.praeger.com

Printed in China through World Print Ltd.

The paper used in this book complies with the Permanent Paper Standard issued
by the National Information Standards Organization (Z39.48-1984).

10 9 8 7 6 5 4 3 2 1

CONTENTS

Key to Map Symbols

Army	XXXX ⊠	Brigade	X ⊠	Infantry	⊠
Corps	XXX ⊠	Regiment	III ⊠	Cavalry	◨
Division	XX ⊠	Battalion	II ⊠	Artillery	[•]

The Strategic Situation, June to September 1863

1-3 July:
Battle of Gettysburg
ends Lee's invasion
of the North

OHIO   PENNSYLVANIA

NEW
JERSEY

Sharpsburg

ILLINOIS   INDIANA

WEST
VIRGINIA

MARYLAND

DELAWARE

Washington

St Louis

KENTUCKY

Fredericksburg

Richmond

MISSOURI

Ohio

Appomattox
CH

Nashville

Initial positions of the
Army of the Cumberland
and the Army of
Tennessee in June 1863

VIRGINIA

Petersburg

ARKANSAS

TENNESSEE

Murfreesboro

Buckner's Corps
reinforce Bragg

9 September:
Longstreet's Corps
en route to
reinforce Bragg

Memphis

Chattanooga

NORTH CAROLINA

*Chickamauga
Creek*

ALABAMA

GEORGIA

SOUTH
CAROLINA

Atlanta

Confederacy

0   50   100 Miles

0   80   160 Km

4 July: Vicksburg
surrenders to Grant

MISSISSIPPI

Vicksburg

LOUISIANA

4 September:
Walker's division
en route to
reinforce Bragg

New
Orleans

▼ *The night of 9/10
September: Rosecrans
allows his troops to become
scattered in their pursuit.
Thomas, lacking any
cavalry screen, sends
Negley into McClemore's
Cove where he stands
isolated and vulnerable.
Bragg tries to pounce on
Negley, only to be foiled
by balky subordinates.
Alerted to his danger,
Rosecrans begins to
concentrate his army.*

Rosecrans' Advance to the Chickamauga Battlefield

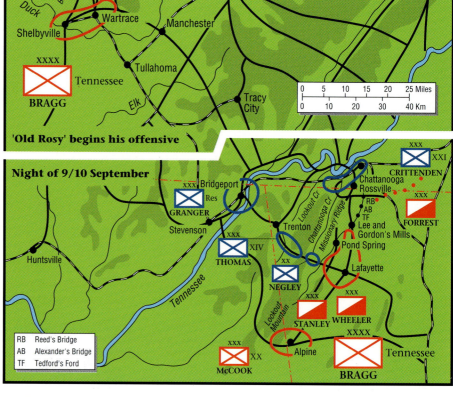

XXXX
The
Cumberland

ROSECRANS

Murfreesboro

Guy's Gap

Bellbuckle Gap

Liberty Gap

Hoover's Gap

Mc Minnville

Duck

Wartrace

Manchester

Shelbyville

XXXX

Tennessee

Tullahoma

BRAGG

Elk

Tracy
City

0   5   10   15   20   25 Miles

0   10   20   30   40 Km

'Old Rosy' begins his offensive

▲▶ *After a seven-month
rest and refit following the
Battle of Murfreesboro,
Rosecrans begins a
cleverly conceived
offensive on 26 June 1863.
While feinting through the
gaps on his right, Wilder's
brigade seizes Hoover's
Gap, allowing Thomas to
outflank Bragg's position.
After reaching
Manchester, Rosecrans
tries to seize the crossings
of the River Elk behind
Tullahoma. Bragg eludes
the trap but has to retreat
across the River
Tennessee. In nine days of
skilful manoeuvre
Rosecrans has cleared
central Tennessee.*

Night of 9/10 September

XXX   XXI
CRITTENDEN

Chattanooga
Rossville

xxx   Bridgeport
Res

RB
AB
TF

XXX

GRANGER

Lookout Cr

Missionary Ridge

Chattanooga Cr

FORREST

Stevenson

Trenton

Lee and
Gordon's Mills

XXX

XIV

Pond Spring

THOMAS

XX

Lafayette

Huntsville

XXX

NEGLEY

Tennessee

Lookout
Mountain

XXX

XXX

STANLEY   WHEELER

XXXX

Alpine

Tennessee

RB   Reed's Bridge
AB   Alexander's Bridge
TF   Tedford's Ford

XXX   XX

BRAGG

McCOOK

BACKGROUND TO BATTLE

In mid-summer 1863 the end appeared near for the Confederate States of America. Lee had returned from Gettysburg, his army mauled and shaken. Grant had captured Vicksburg; the River Mississippi ran 'unvexed to the sea'. In the crucial middle ground in Tennessee, Union General William Rosecrans stood poised to advance on Chattanooga, the gateway to the Confederate heartland.

The commander-in-chief of the Confederate military, President Jefferson Davis, reassessed strategic options. He invited his most trusted general, Robert E. Lee, to Richmond for a conference. Lee favoured another try in Virginia. His senior Lieutenant General, James B. Longstreet, disagreed. Longstreet wrote: 'I know but little of the condition of our affairs in the west, but am inclined to the opinion that our best opportunity for great results is in Tennessee.' Longstreet's ignorance of 'affairs in the west' was an affliction infecting the entire Confederate high command. Congressmen representing the western Confederacy charged that the Davis government overly ignored the west and concentrated too much attention and resources in Virginia. They maintained that in consequence the Mississippi River had been lost. More recently, General Braxton Bragg, the commander of the Army of Tennessee, had been manoeuvred out of Tennessee. But proponents of a western strategy lacked Lee's stature. As a Virginian, Lee, in turn, had great difficulty in looking beyond his beloved state's defence, and as a consequence his fixation on Virginia dominated the strategic mentality of the government in Richmond. Then came Gettysburg.

Following that terrible defeat, the western lobby gained Davis' ear. The government paid attention when Longstreet proposed going on the defensive in Virginia so as to allow one infantry corps to be transferred west to Tennessee. Longstreet even hinted strongly that Bragg lacked the confidence of his men and that he, Longstreet, should go west to replace him. This step was more than Davis could accept. Instead, Davis asked Lee if he would take command in Tennessee. Lee was reluctant, and upon further reflection Davis too questioned such a transfer. Lee held a mastery over the Federal generals who dared to invade Virginia. His skill would be particularly needed if his army were weakened by the transfer of substantial forces to Tennessee. Looking disaster squarely in the eye, Davis embarked upon a colossal strategic gamble: he would reinforce Bragg by stripping forces from all the other major Confederate armies. Thus strengthened, Bragg would try to destroy Rosecrans' army and reverse the tide flowing against the Confederacy. Longstreet would go west with two divisions, not as a replacement for Bragg, but to help him regain Tennessee. As Longstreet mounted his horse to depart, Lee said, 'Now, general, you must beat those people out in the West.' Longstreet replied, 'If I live; but I would not give a single man of my command for a fruitless victory.'

The Confederate Army of Tennessee was indeed a hard-luck outfit. Following the battle of Shiloh in 1862 the defeated army retreated to Corinth to reorganize. Two events coincided to mark the western army with misfortune: Bragg rose to the top command, and the one-year enlistments ran out. Many who had patriotically volunteered wanted to go home. Instead they found themselves conscripted for the duration. For this injustice they blamed Bragg, although he had nothing to do with the decision. An enlisted man recalls that henceforth, '. . . a soldier was simply a machine, a conscript . . . We cursed Bragg, we cursed the Southern Confederacy. All our pride and valor had gone and we were sick of war.'

A charismatic leader could have overcome such attitudes, but when Bragg began to impose his stern discipline on the unhappy ranks their morale plummeted. For crimes ranging from desertion and sleeping on guard to departing the ranks for a short visit home, Bragg ordered men to be shot or whipped and branded. He restored discipline – an English tourist, Colonel Free-mantle, called this army the best disciplined in the Confederacy – but only at the price of crushing his men's spirits. They neither loved nor respected

him. Furthermore, events would show him to be a poor provider for his mens' basic needs. Hunger was a constant companion for the soldiers of the Army of Tennessee.

Yet they fought with amazing courage. In blundering stand-up fights, most recently at Murfreesboro in December 1862, they traded casualties with their opponents at a rate that was proportionally much bloodier than the more famous battles in the east. It went for nought. Letters to the soldiers from their families under-

scored the sense of despair. A family letter of an Arkansas colonel said, 'It has been a gloomy and ill-boding summer to the Confederate cause and Army. God only knows what is to be the result.' Indeed, what the soldiers gained on the battlefield seemed to be sacrificed by the strategic incapacity of their leaders.

The command dissension stemming from battlefield defeats tore the army apart. After Murfreesboro Bragg and his top subordinates – most notably generals Polk, Hardee and Breckin-ridge – feuded instead of preparing a defence of middle Tennessee. Even after substantial rein-forcements had arrived, the consequences of previous command dissent remained an uneasy spectre in the background. Kentuckian Simon Buckner arrived to command a new corps. He quickly assumed Breckinridge's role as leader of the implacably anti-Bragg clique. Daniel Harvey Hill replaced Hardee. Hill was irascible and quick to take affront, in other words he was much like Bragg. It was inevitable that the two would have at best an uneasy relationship. From Virginia came Longstreet, never the easiest of subordinates. Longstreet had read about Murfreesboro in the Richmond press and thereby developed a strong bias against Bragg. As if these strong personalities were not enough to cripple Bragg, in August Breckinridge returned. In sum, as the army began the Chickamauga campaign, the anti-Bragg group was near its apogee.

Since the Christmas of 1861 Federal com-manders in the west had understood the vital importance of Tennessee. At that time General Henry Halleck had announced that the army's 'true line of operations' required a move through Tennessee. Progress had been slow. The most recent Union advance had been arrested at Mur-freesboro. For the subsequent seven months Rosecrans rested and refitted his Army of the Cumberland. Then he launched a cleverly con-ceived quick-striking offensive that cleared several mountain and river barriers and captured the key town of Chattanooga. Over-confident, Rosecrans allowed his army to become scattered in pursuit. Simultaneously, Bragg received substantial rein-forcements.

Bragg planned to attack and overwhelm isol-ated elements of Rosecrans' army. His strategy was good but the execution was lamentable. On 11 September 1863 and again on the 13th, Bragg's subordinates balked and thereby permitted the Union troops to escape. These failures angered

◀ *The Battle of Murfreesboro (Stones River) pitted 33,500 rebel infantrymen and gunners against 40,100 Yankees. Each side lost about 12,000 men. This staggering rate of losses – 35 and 30 per cent respectively – was in sharp contrast to those of the battles fought in the east. (US Library of Congress)*

Bragg. Worse, the close calls alerted his opponent to his danger. Rosecrans ordered his corps to concentrate. By 17 September Rosecrans' four corps lay along a 20-mile front on the west bank of Chickamauga Creek. Bragg's better concentrated army was on the opposite bank. Refusing to relinquish the initiative, Bragg resolved to cross the creek and strike a blow before Rosecrans could concentrate further. He planned to advance against the Union left and thus cut off three Yankee corps from their base at Chattanooga. Rosecrans, correctly divining Bragg's strategy, ordered forced marches to reinforce his left. On the evening of 18 September the two great rival armies massed on what would become the greatest western battlefield of the war.

◀ *A British visitor described Braxton Bragg, a West Point graduate and Mexican War hero, as 'the least prepossessing of the Confederate generals'. He was thin, stoop-shouldered and of a cadaverous, haggard appearance. Only his bright, piercing eyes indicated his inner fire. A private observed him and said, '... his countenance shows marks of deep and long continued study ... he is a remarkable-looking man, and what I would call a hard case'. A harsh disciplinarian, hated by many of his men, he was unsurpassed in preparing a Confederate army for campaign. Capable of devising sound strategies, he was incapable of earning subordinate loyalty. On the battlefield, when things began to go awry, he proved inflexible. Most of his battles ended in naked frontal assaults upon well-defended Union positions. (Library of Congress)*

OPPOSING COMMANDERS AND THEIR ARMIES

The Army of the Cumberland

A West Point graduate, General William Rosecrans was 43 years old when he fought at Chickamauga. In September 1863 he had an unblemished record of success which had begun with a minor victory over Lee at Rich Mountain in western Virginia. Thereafter he had been transferred west and fought successfully at Iuka and Corinth. Promoted to command the Army of the Cumberland, he became very popular with his men who called him 'Old Rosy'. At Murfreesboro his tenacity had earned him victory over Bragg's Army of Tennessee. Most of his army were veterans of that battle.

The Army of the Cumberland comprised three line and one reserve corps. Major General George H. Thomas commanded the army's largest formation, the four-division XIV Corps with some 23,000 effectives. Major Generals Alexander McCook and Thomas Crittenden commanded XX and XXI Corps, respectively. Each corps had three divisions, McCook's with 13,000 and Crittenden's with 12,000 men. All the divisions of these three corps had three brigades. Major General Gordon Granger led the Reserve Corps, which was really

▶ A 43-year-old West Point graduate, William S. Rosecrans was very popular with his men who called him 'Old Rosy'. He commanded at Murfreesboro where his tenacity earned him victory over Bragg. An excellent strategist, personally brave, reputed to be a heavy drinker and known to be heartily profane, his excitable personality impaired his battlefield ability. (Library of Congress)

UNION ORDER OF BATTLE: FORCES PRESENT AT CHICKAMAUGA

Army of the Cumberland: Maj Gen William S. Rosecrans

General Headquarters: 10th Ohio Infantry; 15th Pennsylvania Cavalry

XIV Army Corps

Maj Gen George H. Thomas

Provost guard 9th Michigan Infantry
Escort: 1st Ohio Cavalry, Company 'L'

XX Army Corps

Maj Gen Alexander McD. McCook

Provost guard 81st Indiana Infantry, Company 'H'
Escort: 2nd Kentucky Cavalry, Company 'I'

1st Division

Brig Gen Absalom Baird

1st Bde:
Col Benjamin F. Scribner
38th Indiana; 2nd Ohio; 33rd Ohio
94th Ohio; 10th Wisconsin
1st Michigan Light Artillery, Btty 'A'

2nd Bde:
Brig Gen John C. Starkweather
24th Illinois; 79th Pennsylvania
1st Wisconsin; 21st Wisconsin
Indiana Light Artillery, 4th Btty

3rd Bde:
Brig Gen John H. King
15th United States, 1st Battalion
16th United States, 1st Battalion
18th United States, 1st Battalion
18th United States, 2nd Battalion
19th United States, 1st Battalion
5th US Artillery, Btty 'H'

2nd Division

Maj Gen James S. Negley

1st Bde:
Brig Gen John Beatty
104th Illinois
42nd Indiana; 88th Indiana
15th Kentucky
Bridges' (Illinois) Btty

2nd Bde:
Col Timothy R. Stanley
Col William L. Stoughton
19th Illinois
11th Michigan
18th Ohio
1st Ohio Light Artillery, Btty 'M'

3rd Bde:
Col William Sirwell
37th Indiana
21st Ohio; 74th Ohio
78th Pennsylvania

1st Division

Brig Gen Jefferson C. Davis

2nd Bde:
Brig Gen William P. Carlin
21st Illinois; 38th Illinois
81st Indiana
101st Ohio

3rd Bde:
Col Hans C. Heg
Col John A. Martin
25th Illinois; 35th Illinois
8th Kansas
15th Wisconsin

Artillery:
Capt William A. Hotchkiss
Minnesota Light, 2nd Btty

2nd Division

Brig Gen Richard W. Johnson

1st Bde:
Brig Gen August Willich
89th Illinois; 32nd Indiana
39th Indiana
(mounted infantry, detached)
15th Ohio; 49th Ohio
1st Ohio Light Artillery, Btty 'A'

2nd Bde:
Col Joseph B. Dodge
79th Illinois; 29th Indiana
30th Indiana; 77th Pennsylvania
Ohio Light Artillery, 20th Btty

3rd Bde:
Col Philemon P. Baldwin
Col William W. Berry
6th Indiana; 5th Kentucky
1st Ohio; 93rd Ohio
Indiana Light Artillery, 5th Btty

3rd Division

Brig Gen John M. Brannan

1st Bde:
Col John M. Connell
82nd Indiana
17th Ohio; 31st Ohio
1st Michigan Light Artillery, Btty 'D'

2nd Bde:
Col John D. Croxton
Col William H. Hays
10th Indiana; 74th Indiana
4th Kentucky; 10th Kentucky
14th Ohio
1st Ohio Light Artillery, Btty 'C'

3rd Bde:
Col Ferdinand Van Derveer
87th Indiana
2nd Minnesota
9th Ohio; 35th Ohio
4th US Artillery, Btty 'I'

4th Division

Maj Gen Joseph J. Reynolds

1st Bde:
Col John T. Wilder
(mounted infantry, detached)
92nd Illinois; 98th Illinois
123rd Illinois
17th Indiana; 72nd Indiana
Indiana Light Artillery, 18th Btty

2nd Bde:
Col Edward A. King
Col Milton S. Robinson
68th Indiana; 75th Indiana
101st Indiana
105th Ohio
Indiana Light Artillery, 19th Btty

3rd Bde:
Brig Gen John B. Turchin
18th Kentucky
11th Ohio
36th Ohio; 92nd Ohio
Indiana Light Artillery, 21st Btty

3rd Division

Maj Gen Philip H. Sheridan

1st Bde:
Brig Gen William H. Lytle
Col Silas Miller
36th Illinois; 88th Illinois
21st Michigan
24th Wisconsin
Indiana Light Artillery, 11th Btty

2nd Bde:
Col Bernard Laiboldt
44th Illinois; 73rd Illinois
2nd Missouri; 15th Missouri
1st Missouri Light Artillery, Btty 'G'

3rd Bde:
Col Luther P. Bradley
Col Nathan H. Walworth
22nd Illinois; 27th Illinois
42nd Illinois; 51st Illinois
1st Illinois Light Artillery, Btty 'C'

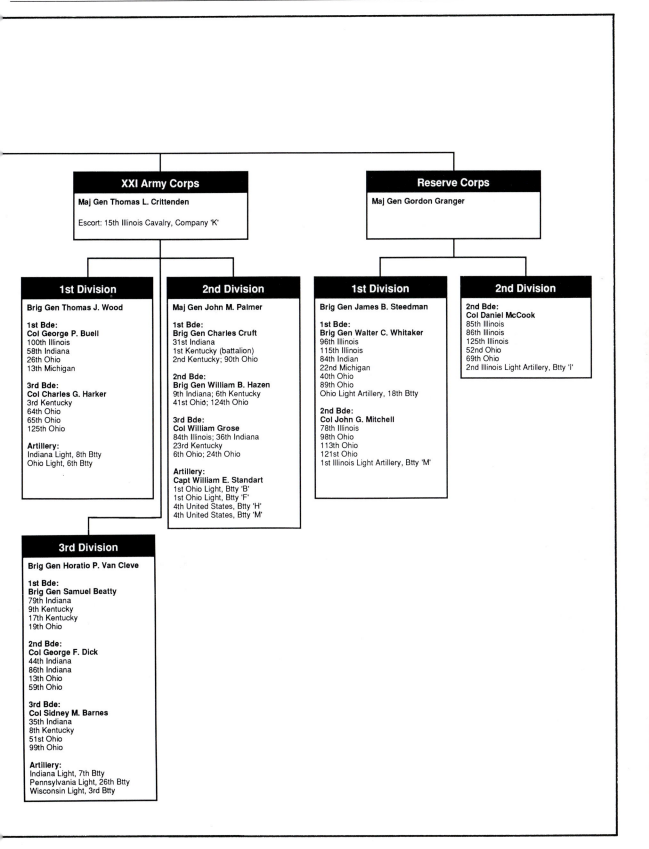

XXI Army Corps

Maj Gen Thomas L. Crittenden

Escort: 15th Illinois Cavalry, Company 'K'

1st Division

Brig Gen Thomas J. Wood

1st Bde:
Col George P. Buell
100th Illinois
58th Indiana
26th Ohio
13th Michigan

3rd Bde:
Col Charles G. Harker
3rd Kentucky
64th Ohio
65th Ohio
125th Ohio

Artillery:
Indiana Light, 8th Btty
Ohio Light, 6th Btty

2nd Division

Maj Gen John M. Palmer

1st Bde:
Brig Gen Charles Cruft
31st Indiana
1st Kentucky (battalion)
2nd Kentucky; 90th Ohio

2nd Bde:
Brig Gen William B. Hazen
9th Indiana; 6th Kentucky
41st Ohio; 124th Ohio

3rd Bde:
Col William Grose
84th Illinois; 36th Indiana
23rd Kentucky
6th Ohio; 24th Ohio

Artillery:
Capt William E. Standart
1st Ohio Light, Btty 'B'
1st Ohio Light, Btty 'F'
4th United States, Btty 'H'
4th United States, Btty 'M'

3rd Division

Brig Gen Horatio P. Van Cleve

1st Bde:
Brig Gen Samuel Beatty
79th Indiana
9th Kentucky
17th Kentucky
19th Ohio

2nd Bde:
Col George F. Dick
44th Indiana
86th Indiana
13th Ohio
59th Ohio

3rd Bde:
Col Sidney M. Barnes
35th Indiana
8th Kentucky
51st Ohio
99th Ohio

Artillery:
Indiana Light, 7th Btty
Pennsylvania Light, 26th Btty
Wisconsin Light, 3rd Btty

Reserve Corps

Maj Gen Gordon Granger

1st Division

Brig Gen James B. Steedman

1st Bde:
Brig Gen Walter C. Whitaker
96th Illinois
115th Illinois
84th Indian
22nd Michigan
40th Ohio
89th Ohio
Ohio Light Artillery, 18th Btty

2nd Bde:
Col John G. Mitchell
78th Illinois
98th Ohio
113th Ohio
121st Ohio
1st Illinois Light Artillery, Btty 'M'

2nd Division

2nd Bde:
Col Daniel McCook
85th Illinois
86th Illinois
125th Illinois
52nd Ohio
69th Ohio
2nd Illinois Light Artillery, Btty 'I'

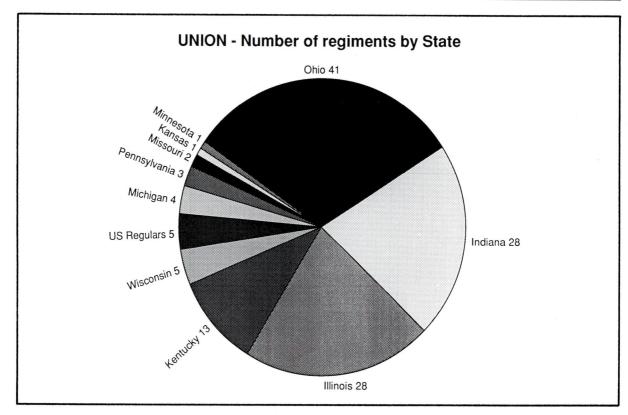

UNION - Number of regiments by State

Ohio 41

Minnesota 1
Kansas 1
Missouri 2
Pennsylvania 3
Michigan 4
US Regulars 5
Wisconsin 5
Kentucky 13
Illinois 28
Indiana 28

These two figures are typical of the appearance of Union Infantry in the field by the late summer of 1863. Long gone are the parade ground spit and polish; the determining factor is now purely practicality. The line officers are dressed little better than the rankers. The Second Lieutenant (left) has a privately-made copy of the issue fatigue blouse which has obviously seen better times, and his shabby appearance is similar to that of the Private alongside him. (Ronald B. Volstad)

an oversized division, with 5,000 men. The army's cavalry corps screened the flanks and did not participate in the battle. Excluding several detached brigades, the army had some 53,000 effective infantry and gunners to fight at Chickamauga.

◀*Rosecrans' army began the campaign in fine fettle. The army's medical director had implemented a new diet and new cooking methods and the men's health improved dramatically. Toiling through the rugged Tennessee and north Georgia terrain required immense stamina. (Tennessee State Library)*

With the exception of a trio of Pennsylvanian units, the army's regiments hailed from the mid- and north-west states of the Union. There was no effort to brigade the regiments according to state. Typically the soldiers were farmers or mechanics. Their ranks included far fewer immigrants than the eastern army's. German immigrants to the Midwest did compose several regiments. The 9th Ohio Regiment, for example, was known as the 'Prussian' regiment. Its men demonstrated the highest devotion to their new country, losing more than half their numbers, the second heaviest regimental loss, at the battle. Scandinavian immigrants composed the 15th Wisconsin. Colonel Heg died at Chickamauga while leading this 'Scandinavian' regiment.

Most soldiers of the Army of the Cumberland carried some version of a rifled musket into battle. A few fortunate companies and the entire crack 21st Ohio carried the five-chambered Colt revolving rifle. Wilder's 'Lightning Brigade' and the 39th Indiana Regiment possessed Spencer seven-shot repeating rifles and fought as mounted infantry.

The Army of Tennessee

The hard centre of Bragg's army comprised those men who had fought with him nine months previously at Murfreesboro. Joining them were a variety of reinforcements. Preston's 5,000-man division had never engaged in a large battle and included an entirely green brigade led by Archibald Gracie. Cheatham's division from east Tennessee, Breckinridge and B. R. Johnson from Mississippi, regiments from various coastal com-

◀ *King's US regulars gave Rosecrans a superb brigade as indicated by this account: 'The regulars charged across a wide, open space and, without firing a shot – drove a superior force of the enemy. The Confederates retreated just in time to prevent us from using the bayonet – the almost invariable result of a bayonet charge pressed home.' (National Archives)*

▲ *Nominally, infantry uniform was dark-blue blouse and kepi and light-blue trousers. But western standards of dress were informal. At very least, most men (including those from the 44th Indiana seen here) discarded the kepi and wore some version of the slouch hat. (US Army Military History Institute)*

mands, and Longstreet's corps from Virginia joined the army prior to the battle. To accommodate these additions, Bragg organized his army into five infantry corps of two divisions each and one additional provisional division commanded by B. R. Johnson. Most divisions had three brigades.

Arriving at accurate comparative strength totals for either army is impossible. Each used a different system of counting, and many records are incomplete. One Confederate brigade, for example, carried into action 2,025 according to its commander Brigadier General Manigault. He mentions that this total excludes 67 soldiers assigned as wagon guards and the infirmary corps of 105 men. Other units included such detachments in their totals. Exclusive of Longstreet's men, Bragg had 40,876 infantry and gunners at the battle. Longstreet added five brigades with about 6,000 men. Like his adversary, Bragg had a cavalry corps screening his flank but it did not participate in the fight. Nathan Bedford Forrest's 3,500 horse soldiers were present, however, and they served as extremely effective mounted infantry. In sum, Bragg had in excess of 50,000 men including 33 foot and four mounted brigades to oppose Rosecrans' 53,000 men who formed 30 foot and one mounted infantry brigade.

Like their opponents, most soldiers in the Army of Tennessee carried a rifled musket, but the Confederates were inferior in all types of equipment. A typical regiment, the 47th Georgia, had separate companies armed with either rifles or muskets. Men of the 5th Tennessee replaced their muskets with Enfields abandoned on the field by the enemy. After the battle ordnance officers complained that the ammunition manufactured by southern arsenals for the Enfield rifle was slightly oversized. This prevented the lubrication of the outside of the cartridge, standard practice for imported Enfield cartridges manufactured in Britain, and thus slowed down loading and increased the chance of fouling. The western Rebel dressed even more informally than his Yankee foe. Free-

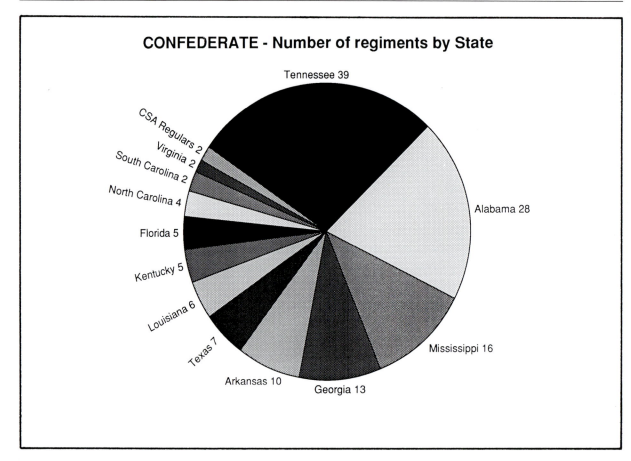

CONFEDERATE - Number of regiments by State

- Tennessee 39
- CSA Regulars 2
- Virginia 2
- South Carolina 2
- North Carolina 4
- Florida 5
- Kentucky 5
- Louisiana 6
- Texas 7
- Arkansas 10
- Georgia 13
- Mississippi 16
- Alabama 28

mantle described the men of Liddell's brigade as 'good sized, healthy, and well clothed' without any uniformity of dress, wearing various shades of grey or brown and felt hats. They preferred their coarse homespun jackets and trousers to government issue uniforms. In contrast, many of Longstreet's men received new grey uniforms during their trip west. The arrival of eastern troops stimulated much interest and mutual jealousy.

Infantry Tactics

The standard of marksmanship in both armies was quite high. A Tennessee private recalls a target shooting competition in which the mark was put some 500 yards' distant. Every marksman hit it. The firing stirred a rabbit which began to run in panic. At a range of 250 yards a soldier shot the rabbit dead. During the battle they put their marksmanship to use. Officers in a Mississippi regiment told the men that they would have to move, because a Yankee sharpshooter was firing and 'killing every time he shot'. A soldier volunteered to get him: 'At first I could not see the man but could see the smoke of his gun, but he soon exposed himself to ram his gun, that was my chance and I fired at him about 125 yards, striking him under the left shoulder-blade.' These were soldiers who could and did hit the man they aimed at when they raised their rifles and 'pulled down' at the target.

Yet the soldiers fired thousands of shots that missed. A Kentucky veteran explains, and also well describes the tactics of a fire fight: 'While ninety per cent of these shots were being fired the men were lying flat on their faces and were overshooting each other when suddenly one or the other would spring to his feet and with a bound and a

◀ *Confederate guerrillas, bushwackers and cavalry raiders were sure to try to interrupt an invader's supply line. These enemies enjoyed detailed knowledge of the terrain and support from the civilian population. One of the most formidable of them, Nathan Forrest,* *explained: 'I know the country perfectly . . . and am well acquainted with all the prominent planters . . . I also have officers in my command . . . who have rafted timber out of the [river] bottoms, and know every foot of ground.' (Tennessee State Library)*

Even more so than in Union armies. Confederate uniforms were a confused mixture of State- and Government-issued equipment combined with personal and looted items. Western theatre armies had even less uniformity than their relatives in the East. This particular 'Reb' is a Private in the 7th Florida Volunteer Infantry, part of Trigg's Brigade of Preston's Division. (Ronald B. Volstad)

◀ *The transfer of Longstreet's Corps from Virginia to Tennessee was a bold attempt to regain the initiative. President Jefferson Davis said, 'I can but hope . . . that with the large army which General Bragg commands he will recover by force the country out of which he seems to have been manoeuvred.' (Tennessee State Library)*

▼ *The departing Virginia troops took a 965-mile circuitous route through* the Carolinas and Georgia. *The railroad gauges were not uniform. At many points the rail lines did not connect, requiring the troops to detrain, proceed by foot, re-entrain and continue. Worn rails and overworked engines and cars limited train speed. Their arrival created quite a stir. A soldier in the 27th Mississippi recalls that they 'passed in high glee, and said they had come to show us how they fought in Virginia'. (Library of Congress)*

Armaments of the Army of Tennessee in March 1863

Infantry

Smooth-bore percussion muskets	11,869
Rifled arms of different calibres	19,942

Cavalry

Smooth-bore percussion muskets	1,363
Rifles of different calibres	4,649
Carbines of different calibres and musketoons	1,469
Double-barrelled guns	773
Pistols (Colt's pattern)	1,566
Pistols (percussion single-barrelled)	42

Field Artillery

12lb light guns	16
6lb guns	40
12lb howitzers	40
Rifled guns, calibre 3.8in*	7
Rifled guns calibre 3.68in*	2
Rifled guns, calibre 3.3in	2
Rifled guns, calibre 3in	11
Rifled guns, calibre 2.9in (Parrott)	6
Ellsworth's breech-loading	1

* taken at Murfreesboro.

yell rush at a double-quick upon their foe, giving him time to fire one or at most two rounds when his ranks would be broken and compelled to retire.' Whether in reserve or in the firing line, soldiers lay down to present smaller targets. If they remained in position for any length of time, they hastily gathered logs, rocks and fence rails to make breastworks for protection against enemy fire. Regimental battle accounts describe how a regiment would shift position and then send a detail back to the former position to carry forward the breastworks so that they could be reused.

As in all battles, the waiting before the conflict began tried nerves the most. A Tennessee soldier wrote, 'The 5th is not (as generals say) eager for the fray, that is a humbug, but willing and not afraid to fight . . . I expected I would be afraid but the firing soon brought on the old battle feeling.' Officers on both sides noted how few straggled from the fight at Chickamauga. A Kentucky soldier spoke for most when he wrote, 'The old veteran needs no one to tell him when a crisis is approaching, he instinctively . . . comprehends the meaning of these movements and nerves himself for the desperate work before him.'

Finally, in both armies an officer's authority was directly related to his battlefield bravery. As one Confederate officer described it, 'every atom

of authority has to be purchased by a drop of your blood'. After two years of active service the citizen volunteers had become veterans and displayed thoroughly professional infantry tactics. To European eyes they did not look polished; Freemantle sniffed that Bragg's men could not form a square on the parade ground, but they knew what they needed to know to survive in combat. They lay down whenever possible, whether in reserve positions or in the front line. They would get up to fire or charge, perform the passage of the lines while under fire, and most impressively, change front and dress ranks while charging at the double and being pelted with rifle and canister fire. They tended to become scattered after a charge and were thus vulnerable to counter-attack. This tendency imparted an ebb and flow to the tactics of a battle.

A description of a typical action, a change of formation under fire and a counter-attack, by the Federal 8th Kentucky exemplifies their skill: 'The colonel ordered "On the right, into line, march!" ... We executed this manoeuvre at the double-quick, with as much precision as we ever did on the drill-field. As soon as Rousseau's men had cleared our front, our boys opened "fire at will". When within sixty yards of the enemy, the order was given and repeated at the top of the voice of every captain: "Fix bayonets, charge!" When we were within twenty yards of the enemy they broke into a perfect rout. The Eighth Kentucky and Fifty-first Ohio boys kept up the charge, firing and re-loading as fast as expert hands could.'

The Artillery

The Army of Tennessee's artillery arsenal which fought at Chickamauga amounted to 31 foot and three and a half cavalry batteries. All gunners in both armies rode into battle which gave the batteries good mobility. Most Rebel batteries had four artillery tubes manned by an average of 91 officers and men. The guns were a thoroughly mixed lot comprising everything from obsolete 6lb smoothbores to modern 3in rifled guns. They included 12 and 24lb howitzers, several of the latter mounted on 6lb carriages so that the shock of repeated firing during the battle caused the

carriage to collapse, and the ubiquitous 12lb Napoleons. Confederate artillery ammunition was inferior, fuzes proved unreliable, shells failed to explode. The friction primers necessary to fire the guns were poorly made and generated complaints after the battle. Some divisions and corps organized the artillery into battalions, others assigned batteries directly to the infantry brigades. There were two army reserve artillery battalions as well.

Union artillery too comprised a mixed bag. A few regular army batteries had four field pieces, with one exception the rest had six each. The battery assigned to Wilder's Brigade of mounted infantry, the 18th Indiana, included six 3in rifled guns and four mountain howitzers. No effort was made to arm a typical six-gun battery with uniform pieces. The smallest common denominator was the two-gun section. Some batteries had three sections armed with three different types of weapon, many had two sections of one type and one of another, while a few had all three sections using the same type of gun. Difficult to describe, it was even more difficult for those officers assigned the task of providing the neccessary variety of ammunition. Thirty Federal batteries engaged during the battle.

Because of the closed terrain around Chickamauga Creek, gunners found few opportunities to support effectively their infantry assaults let alone deploy their guns in any kind of grand battery. On the defensive, dangers abounded because the woods enabled infantry to approach undetected. Thus many batteries suffered the fate described by a soldier in the 19th Ohio: 'We ran full upon the left flank of a Rebel battery heavily supported by infantry. Instantaneously our boys concentrated

Union Artillery by Type Present on the field*	
6lb smoothbore	10
12lb light	16
12lb howitzer	16
12lb Napoleon	46
mountain howitzer	4
3-inch rifled	38
10lb Parrott	28
6lb James rifled	32
24lb howitzer	2
Grand total	192

*Does not include guns serving with cavalry

This Lieutenant-Colonel and the two Privates who accompany him are typical of mid-war Confederate Artillery, although it is unusual to see an officer's sash worn in the field. The Cannon is the 3 in, 10-pdr. 'Parrott rifle', quite possibly captured from Union troops. In the heavily wooded terrain at Chickamauga, this rifled piece would be no more effective than a smoothbore. (Ronald B. Volstad)

CONFEDERATE ORDER OF BATTLE: FORCES PRESENT AT CHICKAMAUGA

Army of Tennessee: Gen Braxton Bragg

Headquarters Escort: Dreux's Company, Louisiana Cavalry; Holloway's Company, Alabama Cavalry

Right Wing

Lieut Gen Leonidas Polk
Escort:
Greenleaf's Company,
Louisiana Cavalry

Reserve Corps

Maj Gen William H. T. Walker

Longstreet's Corps

Maj Gen John B. Hood

Left Wing

Lieut Gen James Longstreet

Cheatham's Division

Maj Gen Benjamin F. Cheatham
Escort:
Company 'G', 2nd Georgia Cavalry

Jackson's Bde:
Brig Gen John K. Jackson
1st Georgia (Confederate), 2nd Btn
5th Georgia
2nd Georgia Btn Sharpshooters
5th Mississippi; 8th Mississippi

Smith's Bde:
Brig Gen Preston Smith
Col Alfred J. Vaughan, Jr.
11th Tennessee
12th & 47th Tennessee
13th & 154th Tennessee
29th Tennessee
Dawson's Sharpshooters

Maney's Bde:
Brig Gen George Maney
1st & 27th Tennessee
4th Tennessee (Provisional Army)
6th & 9th Tennessee
24th Tennessee Btn Sharpshooters

Wright's Bde:
Brig Gen Marcus J. Wright
8th Tennessee; 16th Tennessee
28th Tennessee; 38th Tennessee
51st & 52nd Tennessee

Strahl's Bde:
Brig Gen Otho F. Strahl
4th & 5th Tennessee
19th Tennessee; 24th Tennessee
31st Tennessee; 33rd Tennessee

Artillery:
Maj Melancthon Smith
Carnes' (Tennessee) Battery
Scogin's (Georgia) Battery
Scott's (Tennessee) Battery
Smith's (Mississippi) Battery
Stanford's (Mississippi) Battery

Walker's Division

Brig Gen States R. Gist

Gist's Bde:
Brig Gen States R. Gist
Col Peyton H. Colquitt
Lieut Col Leroy Napier
46th Georgia; 8th Georgia Battalion
24th South Carolina

Ector's Bde:
Brig Gen Matthew D. Ector
Stone's (Alabama) Battalion
Sharpshooters
Pound's (Mississippi) Battalion
Sharpshooters
29th North Carolina; 9th Texas
10th Texas Cavalry
14th Texas Cavalry
32nd Texas Cavalry

Wilson's Bde:
Col Claudius C. Wilson
25th Georgia; 29th Georgia
30th Georgia
1st Georgia Btn Sharpshooters
4th Louisiana Battalion

Artillery:
Howell's (Georgia) Battery

Liddell's Division

Brig Gen St. John R. Liddell

Liddell's Bde:
Col Daniel C. Govan
2nd & 15th Arkansas
5th & 13th Arkansas
6th & 7th Arkansas; 8th Arkansas
1st Louisiana (Regulars)

Walthall's Bde:
Brig Gen Edward C. Walthall
24th Mississippi; 27th Mississippi
29th Mississippi; 30th Mississippi
34th Mississippi

Artillery: Capt Charles Swett
Fowler's (Alabama) Battery
Warren Light Artillery
(Mississippi Battery)

Hindman's Division

Maj Gen Thomas C. Hindman
Brig Gen Patton Anderson
Escort:
Lenoir's Company, Alabama Cavalry

Anderson's Bde:
Brig Gen Patton Anderson
Col J. H. Sharp
7th Mississippi; 9th Mississippi
10th Mississippi; 41st Mississippi
44th Mississippi
9th Mississippi Btn Sharpshooters
Garrity's (Alabama) Battery

Deas' Bde:
Brig Gen Zach C. Deas
19th Alabama; 22nd Alabama
25th Alabama; 39th Alabama
50th Alabama
17th Alabama Btn Sharpshooters
Dent's (Alabama) Battery

Manigault's Bde:
Brig Gen Arthur M. Manigault
24th Alabama; 28th Alabama
34th Alabama
10th & 19th South Carolina
Waters' (Alabama) Battery

Hood's Division

Maj Gen John B. Hood
Brig Gen E. McIver Law

Law's Bde:
Brig Gen E. McIver Law
Col James L. Sheffield
4th Alabama; 15th Alabama
44th Alabama; 47th Alabama
48th Alabama

Robertson's Bde:
Brig Gen Jerome B. Robertson
Col Van H. Manning
3rd Arkansas
1st Texas; 4th Texas; 5th Texas

Benning's Bde:
Brig Gen Henry L. Benning
2nd Georgia; 15th Georgia
17th Georgia; 20th Georgia

McLaws' Division

Brig Gen Joseph B. Kershaw
Maj Gen Lafayette McLaws

Kershaw's Bde:
Brig Gen Joseph B. Kershaw
2nd South Carolina
3rd South Carolina
7th South Carolina
8th South Carolina
15th South Carolina
3rd South Carolina Battalion

Humphreys' Bde:
Brig Gen Benjamin G. Humphreys
13th Mississippi
17th Mississippi
18th Mississippi
21st Mississippi

Reserve Artillery

Maj Felix H. Robertson
Barret's (Missouri) Battery
Le Gardeur's (Louisiana) Battery
Havis' (Georgia) Battery
Lumsden's (Alabama) Battery
Massenburg's (Georgia) Battery

Hill's Corps

Lieut Gen Daniel H. Hill

Buckner's Corps

Maj Gen Simon B. Buckner
Escort:
Clark's Company, Tennessee Cavalry

Forrest's Corps

Brig Gen Nathan B. Forrest
Escort:
Jackson's Company, Tennessee Cavalry

Cleburne's Division

Maj Gen Patrick R. Cleburne
Escort:
Sanders' Company,
Tennessee Cavalry

Wood's Bde:
Brig Gen S. A. M. Wood
16th Alabama; 33rd Alabama
45th Alabama
18th Alabama Battalion
32nd & 45th Mississippi
15th Mississippi Btn Sharpshooters

Polk's Bde:
Brig Gen Lucius E. Polk
1st Arkansas
3rd & 5th Confederate
2nd Tennessee; 35th Tennessee
48th Tennessee

Deshler's Bde:
Brig Gen James Deshler
Col Roger Q. Mills
19th & 24th Arkansas
6th & 10th Texas Infantry/
15th Texas Cavalry
17th, 18th, 24th, 25th Texas Cavalry

Artillery:
Maj T. R. Hotchkiss
Capt Henry C. Semple
Calvert's (Arkansas) Battery
Douglas' (Texas) Battery
Semple's (Alabama) Battery

Breckinridge's Division

Maj Gen John C. Breckinridge
Escort:
Foules' Company,
Mississippi Cavalry

Helm's Bde:
Brig Gen Benjamin H. Helm
Col Joseph H. Lewis
41st Alabama
2nd Kentucky; 4th Kentucky
6th Kentucky; 9th Kentucky

Adams' Bde:
Brig Gen Daniel W. Adams
Col Randall L. Gibson
32nd Alabama
13th & 20th Louisiana
16th & 25th Louisiana
19th Louisiana
14th Louisiana Battalion

Stovall's Bde:
Brig Gen Marcellus A. Stovall
1st & 3rd Florida
4th Florida
47th Georgia
60th North Carolina

Artillery: Maj Rice E. Graves
Cobb's (Kentucky) Battery
Graves' (Kentucky) Battery
Mebane's (Tennessee) Battery
Slocomb's (Louisiana) Battery

Armstrong's Division

Brig Gen Frank C. Armstrong

Armstrong's Bde:
Col James T. Wheeler
3rd Arkansas; 2nd Kentucky
6th Tennessee; 18th Tennessee

Forrest's Bde:
Col George G. Dibrell
4th Tennessee; 8th Tennessee
9th Tennessee; 10th Tennessee
11th Tennessee
Shaw's & O. P. Hamilton's Btn/
R. D. Allison's Squadron
Huggins' (Tennessee) Battery
Morton's (Tennessee) Battery

Pegram's Division

Brig Gen John Pegram

Davidson's Bde:
Brig Gen H. B. Davidson
1st Georgia; 6th Georgia
6th North Carolina
Rucker's (1st Tennessee) Legion
Huwald's (Tennessee) Battery

Scott's Bde: Col John S. Scott
10th Confederate
det of John H. Morgan's command
1st Louisiana; 2nd Tennessee
5th Tennessee
N. T. N. Robinson's (Louisiana) Btty
(1 section)

Preston's Division

Brig Gen William Preston

Gracie's Bde:
Brig Gen Archibald Gracie, Jr
43rd Alabama
1st Alabama Battalion
2nd Alabama Battalion
3rd Alabama Battalion
4th Alabama Battalion
63rd Tennessee

Trigg's Bde:
Col Robert C. Trigg
1st Florida Cavalry
6th Florida
7th Florida
54th Virginia

Third Bde:
Col John H. Kelly
65th Georgia
5th Kentucky
58th North Carolina
63rd Virginia

Artillery Battalion:
Maj A. Leyden
Jeffress' (Virginia) Battery
Peeples' (Georgia) Battery
Wolihin's (Georgia) Battery

Stewart's Division

Maj Gen Alexander P. Stewart

Johnson's Bde:
Brig Gen Bushrod R. Johnson
Col John S. Fulton
17th Tennessee; 23rd Tennessee
25th Tennessee; 44th Tennessee

Bate's Bde:
Brig Gen William B. Bate
58th Alabama; 37th Georgia
4th Georgia Btn Sharpshooters
15th & 37th Tennessee
20th Tennessee

Brown's Bde:
Brig Gen John C. Brown
Col Edmund C. Cook
18th Tennessee; 26th Tennessee
32nd Tennessee; 45th Tennessee
23rd Tennessee Battalion

Clayton's Bde:
Brig Gen Henry D. Clayton
18th Alabama; 36th Alabama
38th Alabama

Artillery:
Maj J. Wesley Eldridge
1st Arkansas Battery
T. H. Dawson's (Georgia) Battery
Eufaula Artillery (Alabama) Battery
Company 'E',
9th Georgia Artillery Battalion

Reserve Corps Artillery

Maj Samuel C. Williams
Baxter's (Tennessee) Battery
Darden's (Mississippi) Battery
Kolb's (Alabama) Battery
McCants' (Florida) Battery

Johnson's Division

Brig Gen Bushrod R. Johnson

Gregg's Bde:
Brig Gen John Gregg
Col Cyrus A. Sugg
3rd Tennessee; 10th Tennessee
30th Tennessee; 41st Tennessee
50th Tennessee
1st Tennessee Battalion; 7th Texas
Bledsoe's (Missouri) Battery

McNair's Bde:
Brig Gen Evander McNair
Col David Coleman
1st Arkansas Mounted Rifles
2nd Arkansas Mounted Rifles
25th Arkansas
4th & 31st Arkansas and
4th Arkansas Battalion
39th North Carolina
Culpeper's (South Carolina) Battery

their fire upon this and with a shower of lead drove the Rebel gunners and their support from their pieces.' Rendered immobile after having its horses shot down, the battery fell to the subsequent infantry charge.

Cavalry

Cavalry tactics were similiar on both sides. The wooded, broken terrain made mounted charges rare. Typically troopers rode into battle, left their horses at some convenient place – one horseholder remained behind to hold his and three other horses – in Forrest's cavalry the ratio was one to five – and performed as infantry skirmishers. They remained close to their horses so that they could quickly remount and retreat or pursue or transfer to another sector of the field. Observing some Confederate cavalry skirmishers, Freemantle commented that their horse management 'was very pretty'.

Medical

Medical practice during the war has usually been portrayed as having been primitive. Although both armies had their share of unskilled surgeons and drunkards who bloodily plunged into frenzies of amputations, they also had many thoughtful practitioners who tried to provide the best possible care. The factor most hindering their efforts was ignorance of bacteriology. The brightest among them recognized some link between sanitation, both in camp and during surgery, and well-being. Medical personnel in the Army of the Cumberland appreciated the dangers posed by the overcrowding of wounded men and tried to alleviate conditions in this area. They realized the benefits of quick surgical intervention following a wound. Rosecrans' medical director reported with sorrow

▼*Union ability, exemplified by the 1st Michigan Engineers and Mechanics, to build bridges and rail lines (here across the Tennessee River at Chattanooga) contributed immensely to Old Rosy's capture of Chattanooga. (US Army Military History Institute)*

Mounted charges by Cavalry were a relatively rare occurence in the Civil War. It was far more usual for them to be employed as scouts, skirmishers, raiders or at best mounted infantry. In the broken terrain of the Chickamauga valley mounted engagements were even less likely but the fighting was as bitter as ever. (Ronald B. Volstad)

that the retreat from the battlefield caused many with knee and ankle injuries to die unneccessarily because amputations had to be postponed until the wounded reached Chattanooga.

Much depended upon the vigilance of commanding officers. In Thomas's well-managed corps, medical personnel inspected all regiments and batteries before campaigning began, to verify that they had abundant supplies of medicines and surgical instruments. In addition, the corps had a reserve supply consisting of 'hospital tents, blankets, sheets, hair pillows, shirts, drawers, bed-sacks, surgical instruments, bandages, lint, mess-chests, concentrated milk and beef, liquor, chloro-form' and other items 'experience has taught to be most needed and useful' in field emergencies. Rosecrans' medical men were much better supplied with everything, particularly concentrated foods and chloroform, than were Bragg's.

Battlefield Terrain

A mixed-wood forest covered most of the ground west of Chickamauga Creek. One participant called the rough and broken country, 'a dark wilderness of woods and vines and overhanging limbs'. In the frontier style the local farmers – the Poe, Dyer, Snodgrass and Brotherton families – had fenced in their yards and fields and allowed their livestock to range freely outside these fences. Over time the livestock had trampled and grazed many shrubs and brambles leaving the spaces between the trees free from underbrush. Here typical sightlines extended out some 125 to 150 yards on a clear sunny day. Once the light began to fail, either from cloying gun smoke caught beneath the tree canopy or as the sun began to go down, visibility dramatically declined. Throughout the forest dense tangles of vegetation blocked visibility and impaired movement. A Confederate battery commander described how he had to keep his guns a mere 100 yards behind the advancing infantry in order to keep them in view. The open forest did permit the passage of artillery batteries but the terrain greatly restricted the guns' field of fire. After the battle the Union army's Medical Director observed that the proportion of rifle to

cannon wounds was much higher than usual, a fact he attributed to the undulating, forested terrain.

Command and Control

Fighting in woodland posed near insurmountable command and control difficulties. Frequently regi-

mental commanders could not see their entire line of battle; those higher up the chain of command could see only fragments of their command. Officers knew how important it was that their troops maintain alignment; to do otherwise risked a dangerous enfilade fire. This came about when a sector of a defending line did not confront opponents directly to its front. It could then fire to the side, concentrating against the enemy's dangling, exposed flanks. Yet in the wooded terrain along Chickamauga Creek it was often impossible

▼ *Typical campaign terrain. (US National Archives)*

This Sergeant of the 2nd Infantry wears the full dress, single-breasted, frock-coat (double-breasted for field officers) piped in branch-of-service-colour (Infantry light-blue) with brass shoulder-scales. He wears the 'Hardee' hat which, though smart in appearance, was a universally hated item. These were generally replaced as soon as possible with the kepi or slouch hat. This full dress ideal was of no practical use and the appearance of any infantryman in the field would rapidly degenerate to the state of affairs illustrated on p. 15. (Shirley Mallinson)

▼ Federal soldiers enjoying a break during the march. A Florida gunner wrote that Longstreet's men, '. . . say that New England Yankees do not fight as these men do'. But one of Longstreet's Texans wrote, 'I see no difference between this army and the Yanks we met in Virginia.' (Library of Congress)

to preserve proper alignment. A Confederate colonel well describes the problem. Ordered to dress to his right: 'I soon discovered that the arrangement and advance of the line was irregular, and that Polk's brigade was moving with great rapidity and gaining on me to the right. I then began to incline to the right as rapidly as I could to keep a good line, but before I could join on to the left of Polk's brigade . . . my skirmishers were hotly engaged.' The colonel lost sight of Polk as the fight to his front commanded his attention. Consequently both his brigade and Polk's suffered deadly enfilade fire on their exposed flanks. Time and again during the two-day battle it was enfilade fire that broke a defending line or shot an attack to bits.

The ground was entirely unfamiliar to the Union forces. To try to control the fighting, Rosecrans ordered his subordinates to keep in touch with headquarters via a courier chain. The Federal commander also employed his personal escort and a battalion of cavalry as couriers, but as Rosecrans observed with the benefit of hindsight, the system was 'imperfect, and much had to be left to the discretion' of his subordinates. Difficult though it was for the Union high command, at least they were pulling in harness together. Rosecrans had trained his army. It had been together for a year, during which time it had fought two major battles.

The same cannot be said of Bragg's army, a third of whom had joined in the weeks immediately

preceding the battle. Personal animosities divided the Rebel command and the Confederate corps structure was only newly in place and as yet untried. To complicate the chain of command yet farther, when Longstreet reached the battlefield at the end of the first day's fighting, Bragg created an entirely new command structure. Such improvisation impaired Rebel command performance. In partial compensation Confederate generals utilized the services of knowledgeable local guides, including soldiers who were fighting across the fields where they had lived. Finally, one other consideration explains much of what took place. Officers on both sides were extremely short of sleep. Consecutive days of marching in close proximity to the enemy, which involved long hours on duty and intense strain, left everyone 'excessively exhausted' and dull-witted.

▼ *When Bragg evacuated Chattanooga, his men despaired. A soldier in the 22nd Alabama wrote to his sister that 'There is much despondency in the army, many deserters and many others feeling whipped.' When reinforcements came by train, morale soared. A soldier of the* 18th Alabama *in a letter to his family said that 'We have a large army here I don't know how soon we will have to fight. I think we will whip them when we fight.' Seen here is a typical Southern rail depot. (Library of Congress)*

THE FIRST DAY OF BATTLE, 19 SEPTEMBER

On the night of 17 September Bragg issued the orders that initiated the Battle of Chickamauga. Believing that the Union line centred about Lee and Gordon's Mills where a corps commanded by General Crittenden guarded the crossing, he decided that a powerful force comprising three infantry corps would cross Chickamauga Creek, turn left, 'and sweep up the Chickamauga, toward Lee and Gordon's Mill'. As they drove south they would uncover additional fords thereby permitting Polk's and Hill's corps to join the action. Mindful of recent botched opportunities, Bragg ordered

▲ A soldier in the 19th Illinois described the wait before battle: 'It is most trying on the nerves, of even old soldiers, to be held back when the battle is on. But when he can hear a few bullets whistling near him, if he inherits fighting blood it soon begins to circulate; and should he take a part in a successful charge, there is an exultation that makes him forget for a few minutes the comrades who fell on the way. (US Army Military History Institute)

Bragg's Dispositions and Battle Plan

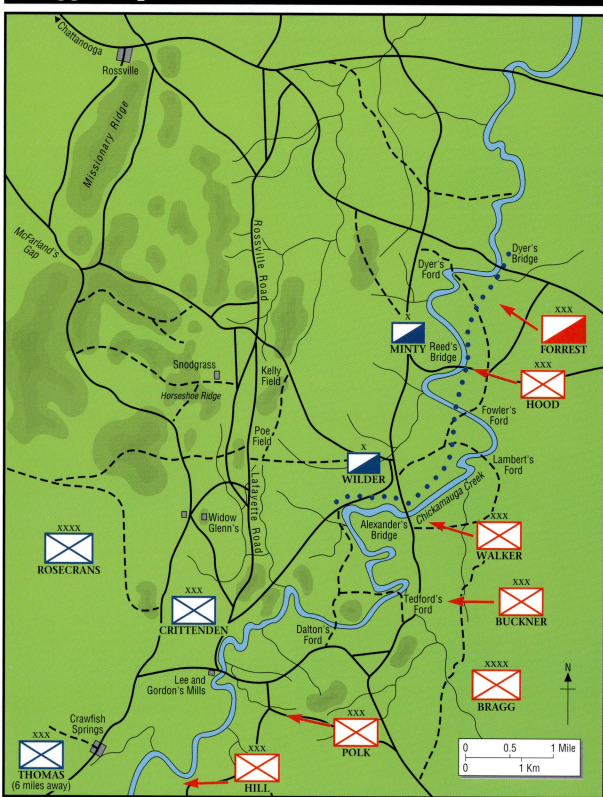

that all movements 'will be executed with the utmost promptness, vigor, and persistence'. Bragg believed that the chosen crossing points for the three corps would place them on the Federal left flank. Thus his attack would drive Rosecrans away from Chattanooga and into a natural cul-de-sac called McLemore's Cove.

On the 18th his columns advanced over the creek. With Crittenden still in position at Lee and Gordon's Mills, Bragg believed that he had set up Rosecrans for a deadly flank attack the next day, but unbeknownst to Bragg, while his men had been marching to attain the Union flank, Rosecrans had anticipated the manoeuvre and gone one better. George Thomas's corps had marched hard and fast all day and into the night, passed through Crittenden's corps and taken up a position on the flank of the intended Confederate flank attack.

▶ *Union cavalry described Reed's bridge as 'a narrow, frail structure . . . planked with loose boards and fence rails'. Union cavalry (seen here) performed a successful counter-reconnaissance action against Forrest on September 18. It was the only useful action performed by Rosecrans' cavalry corps during the battle. (U. Army Military History Institute)*

◀*At dawn on 18 September Bragg's army begin to cross Chickamauga Creek, Crittenden's XXI Corps, positioned at Lee and Gordon's Mills, being their intended objective. Bragg's plan calls for Hood and Walker to cross north of Crittenden, thereby interposing between Rosecrans and Chattanooga (off map to north-west). Once across, Hood and Walker will march south against Crittenden's flank. Thomas's XIV Corps (six miles off map to south-west) force-marches through Crawfish Springs (lower left), passes through Crittenden and takes up positions around the Kelly Field.*

▶ *Lee and Gordon's Mills, from a contemporary illustration.*

The Lafayette Road runs from Lee and Gordon's Mills to Chattanooga. By dawn on 19 September the Union line paralleled this road, extending for five miles in a northward direction from the mills toward Chattanooga. Crittenden's three-division corps occupied the ground nearest the mill while two of Thomas's divisions guarded the Federal left in and about the Kelly field. This field, some three-quarters of a mile long and one-fourth of a mile wide, was on the east side of the road. The ground between the road and Chickamauga Creek was mostly forested with occasional small clearings. Here the battle began.

Thomas had barely arrived at the Kelly field when a subordinate erroneously reported that a single Rebel brigade had crossed the creek and was standing alone and vulnerable. Thomas ordered Brannon's division to attack and destroy this brigade. Brannon drove in Forrest's dismounted cavalry who were screening Walker's infantry crossing the creek, and then encountered Ector's brigade. Hard pressed, Ector told Forrest that he 'was uneasy about his right flank'. Forrest replied, 'Tell General Ector that he need not bother about his right flank. I'll take care of it.' Soon the courier reappeared saying Ector was uneasy about his left

◀ *Liddell's division forced a crossing over Alexander's bridge against the opposition of Wilder's Lightning Brigade seen here. Wilder's fast-shooting mounted infantry obstinately resisted. Liddell reported that he inflicted few losses and suffered 105 casualties, a disproportion he attributed to 'the efficiency of this new weapon' [the Spencer rifle]. (Tennessee State Library)*

◀ *A soldier described the advance through Chickamauga's woods: 'The ground over which we marched was swept by an actual storm of leaden hail – solid shot crashed through the trees or ploughed the ground, while hissing shells exploding made hideous every inch of space. The soil was splashed up in our faces and the limbs and twigs showered upon us from above.' (Tennessee State Library)*

flank. Forrest lost his temper: 'Tell General Ector that by God I am here and will take care of his left flank as well as his right!' Forrest was true to his word. Leading from the front in his customarily fiery style, Forrest had his horse shot from under him. He persevered and when more of Walker's men came up, he joined in a general advance that drove Brannon back to his start-line.

Thomas committed Baird's division to support Brannon. It included the 1,370-man brigade of US regulars who went into action supported by Battery 'H', Fifth Artillery. After a sharp skirmish these fresh troops drove the Rebels back some three-quarters of a mile through the woods. Here the infantry halted while the battery deployed forward to a low ridge. The 16th Infantry lay down behind the battery, and 'without any warning whatever, the Rebels came up on our right flank and got right on us before any disposition could be made to meet them'. The 16th Infantry was nearly eliminated, losing 164 men taken prisoner and escaping with just 67 officers and men of the 308 who had begun. They had been hit by Liddell's division. He had been struggling through the woods when the sound of heavy firing came from his own right rear. Having received orders from Bragg to attack the enemy immediately, Liddell turned northward and marched toward the firing. His men landed squarely on the regulars' flank and delivered a fierce attack. A soldier in the 27th Mississippi recalls: 'we pushed on to the battery that was just beginning to [play] grape and canister on the brigade; but J. S. Thompson, Bill Wofford, Green Westbrook and myself . . . killed the last gunner' and 'bounced astride of a gun and yelled our loudest . . . Every regiment capturing artillery in battle was entitled to the crossed cannon and name of the battle on their regimental flag, and that was a grand inducement to get men to charge batteries where it looked like instant death.'

As the regular brigade fell back, the sight and sound of 15th Infantry's bugler gave them new courage. With a sword in one hand and his bugle in the other, Private William Carson sounded constantly the 'Halt!' and 'Rally!' Spying the flag of the 18th Infantry he sounded 'To the Colour!', ran to the flag himself and formed a one-man rearguard to cover the retreat.

▲ A self-made man lacking formal education, Nathan Bedford Forrest was a private when the war started and a lieutenant general when it ended. He taught his cavalry to fight like no others. Regarding its efforts to hold a bridgehead over the Chickamauga on the 19th, Forrest reported, 'The charges made by Armstrong's division (while fighting on foot) . . . would be creditable to the best drilled infantry.' (Tennessee State Library)

With the Rebels advancing, into the breach at the double came Colonel Kammerling and his 9th Ohio. This was 'a German regiment, using only German language and German tactics'. Seeing the captured artillery Kammerling, on his own initiative, ordered 'Links Schwengket!', swung to the left and charged over the battery. While the Confederates massed for another attack the 9th hastened to rejoin its brigade. This brigade, commanded by Colonel Van Derveer, lay down as fleeing Federal troops poured through their line. Rising at the command, they opened fire. A Union officer described the action: 'The enemy were approaching in orderly array – ranks behind ranks

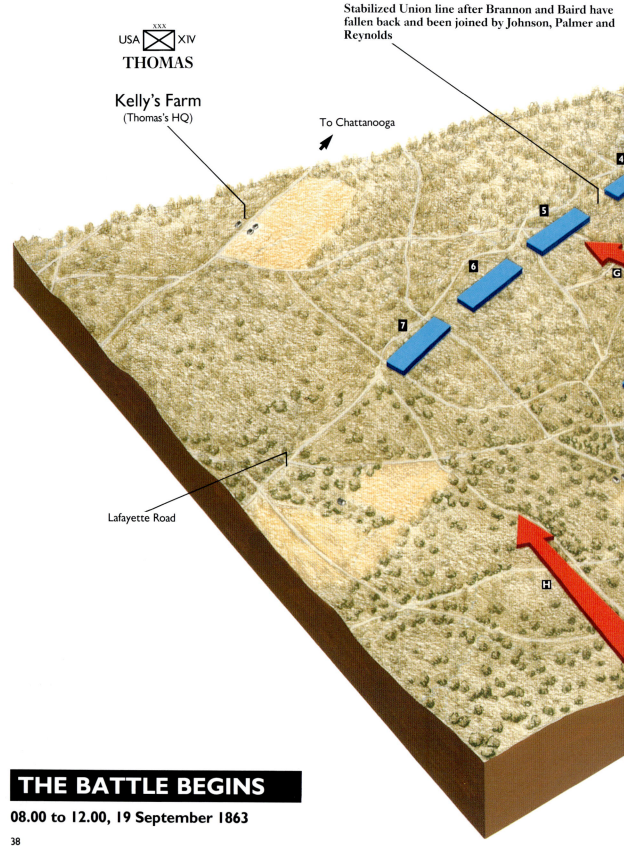

USA ⊠ XIV
xxx
THOMAS

Kelly's Farm
(Thomas's HQ)

Stabilized Union line after Brannon and Baird have
fallen back and been joined by Johnson, Palmer and
Reynolds

To Chattanooga

Lafayette Road

THE BATTLE BEGINS

08.00 to 12.00, 19 September 1863

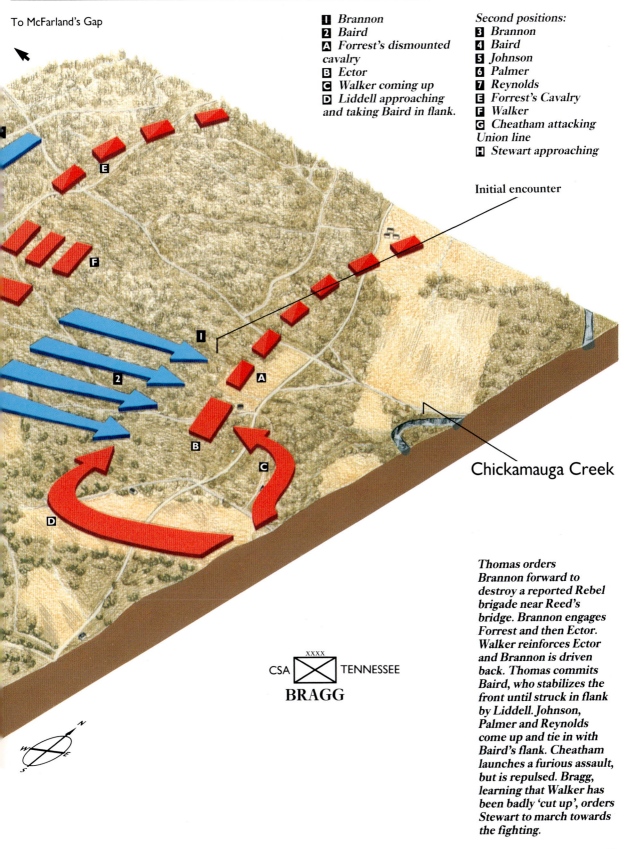

To McFarland's Gap

1 Brannon
2 Baird
A Forrest's dismounted cavalry
B Ector
C Walker coming up
D Liddell approaching and taking Baird in flank.

Second positions:
3 Brannon
4 Baird
5 Johnson
6 Palmer
7 Reynolds
E Forrest's Cavalry
F Walker
G Cheatham attacking Union line
H Stewart approaching

Initial encounter

Chickamauga Creek

CSA ⊠ TENNESSEE

BRAGG

N

Thomas orders Brannon forward to destroy a reported Rebel brigade near Reed's bridge. Brannon engages Forrest and then Ector. Walker reinforces Ector and Brannon is driven back. Thomas commits Baird, who stabilizes the front until struck in flank by Liddell. Johnson, Palmer and Reynolds come up and tie in with Baird's flank. Cheatham launches a furious assault, but is repulsed. Bragg, learning that Walker has been badly 'cut up', orders Stewart to march towards the fighting.

– no skirmishers or preliminary firing, but with the evident intention of forcing an actual collision . . . We opened on them at about 200 yards, with carefully directed file firing, while the battery treated them with canister in double doses. They made no reply, but with splendid courage continued their steady advance. Their ranks were soon so depleted, however, as to make it plain that they could not make a successful rush – at fifty yards they began to "wabble" and commenced firing wildly, and presently they started back in wild disorder.'

These initial encounters established the battle's tone. Because it took place in the woods, fighting would be at short range. It would be full of surprise encounters and sudden opportunistic flank attacks, and weight of numbers would usually decide an issue. It was up to the generals to bring their masses to bear at the decisive points, but because of the command and control problems already described, this was a difficult challenge.

▲*Lieutenant George Van Pelt, commanding the 1st Michigan Battery of six 10lb Parrot rifled guns, was in action during the confused fighting in the woods on the 19th. His battery fired 64 rounds of canister and shell in the* face of the charging Rebels and he 'remained with the battery until the enemy's bayonets were at their breasts'. Van Pelt fell 'like a hero at his post'. (US Army Military History Institute)*

Long afterwards Wilder explained the battle: 'All this talk about generalship displayed on either side is sheer nonsense . . . It was a soldier's fight purely, wherein the only question involved was the question of endurance. The two armies came together like two wild beasts, and each fought as long as it could stand up in a knock-down and drag-out encounter.'

While the action along the Union left was taking place, Rosecrans rode toward the sound of the guns. He arrived at about 1 p.m. and established his headquarters in a small log house occupied by Eliza Glenn, the widow of a Confederate soldier. From the commanding elevation of Widow Glenn's house, Old Rosy supervised the action on the Union right, leaving Thomas to manage affairs on the left. For a while there was only skirmishing in front of Widow Glenn's house, the only upsetting incident being the capture of Rebel soldiers from Hood's division, thus confirming that men from Lee's army had arrived. Then, during the next four hours, three separate assaults by three of Bragg's hardest hitting officers nearly breached Rosecrans' line. The first came from A. P. Stewart's division. Known affectionately to his men as 'Old Straight' – a nickname earned while teaching mathematics and philosophy – Stewart had met Bragg at about noon. Bragg told him that Walker 'was much cut up' and ordered him to march toward the sound of the firing. Stewart, heading through the woods, failed to make contact with any general officers along

Walker's front, and 'fearing to lose too much time' attacked the nearest enemy. 'Old Straight' did not realize it, but he went in a good mile to the left of where Bragg intended him to attack. Here he encountered two brigades of Van Cleve's division.

When the fighting in the woods between Reed's bridge and the Poe field escalated, Thomas had summoned help from Crittenden. Palmer and Van Cleve tied in with Thomas's left flank and counter-attacked. Van Cleve was making good progress – his 79th Indiana and 17th Kentucky had just shot down the horses and half the men of a Rebel battery and then captured the guns – when Stewart appeared 'with terrible force' on the Yankees' flank. There ensued a bitter, bloody, hour-long fight by the end of which Stewart's men had driven Van Cleve to the rear and recaptured the guns. In eager pursuit, Stewart crossed the Lafayette Road and encountered a second Federal position atop a battery-studded rise. This was Rosecrans' headquarters at the Widow Glenn's. It seemed to Stewart's brigadiers that they were about to capture this position as well when they noticed a long Yankee battle line advancing from the south. These were troops of Thomas's remaining division commanded by Negley, which had

▼ Rosecrans (with beard) seated at table with his staff. Unfamiliar with the terrain, Old Rosy enlisted a local widow to help him make sense of the battle. Hearing a burst of fire, he would ask her where it was *and the lady would reply, 'nigh out about Reed's bridge' or 'about a mile fornest John Kelly's house'. It was not a satisfactory system. (US Army Military History Institute)*

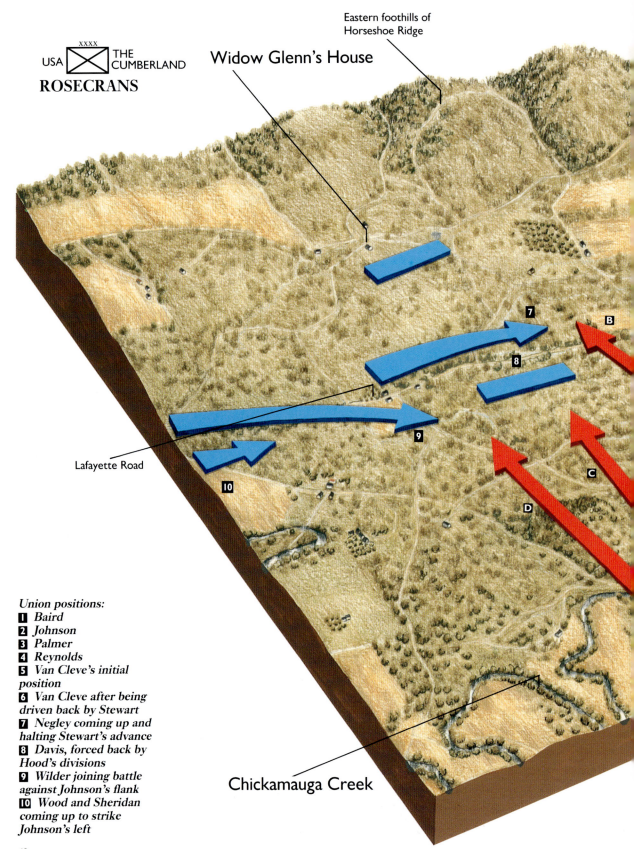

USA ⊠ THE CUMBERLAND
xxxx

ROSECRANS

Eastern foothills of Horseshoe Ridge

Widow Glenn's House

Lafayette Road

Chickamauga Creek

Union positions:
1 *Baird*
2 *Johnson*
3 *Palmer*
4 *Reynolds*
5 *Van Cleve's initial position*
6 *Van Cleve after being driven back by Stewart*
7 *Negley coming up and halting Stewart's advance*
8 *Davis, forced back by Hood's divisions*
9 *Wilder joining battle against Johnson's flank*
10 *Wood and Sheridan coming up to strike Johnson's left*

THREE ASSAULTS ROCK THE UNION POSITION

14.30 to dusk, 19 September 1863

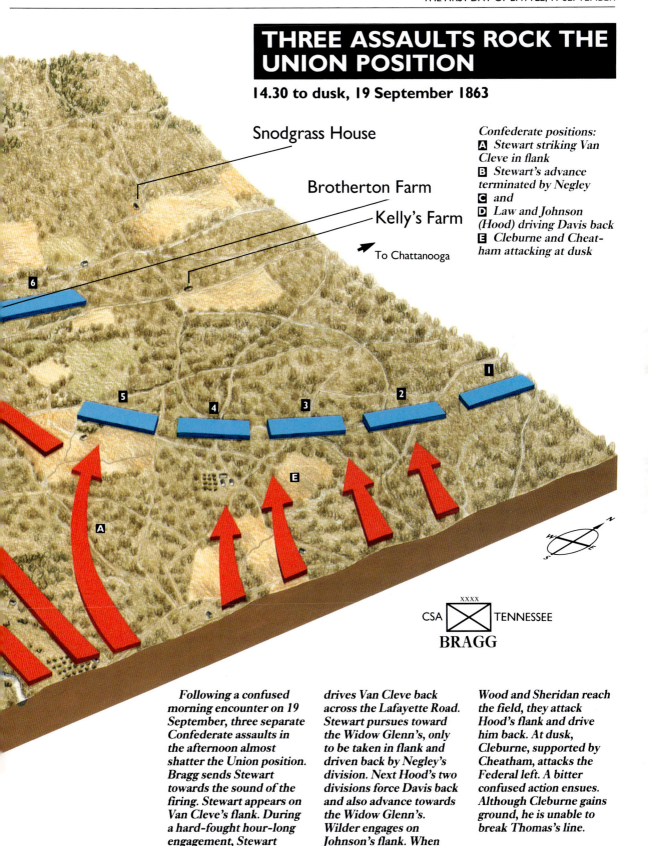

Snodgrass House

Brotherton Farm

Kelly's Farm

To Chattanooga

Confederate positions:
A *Stewart striking Van Cleve in flank*
B *Stewart's advance terminated by Negley*
C *and*
D *Law and Johnson (Hood) driving Davis back*
E *Cleburne and Cheatham attacking at dusk*

CSA ⊠ TENNESSEE
BRAGG

Following a confused morning encounter on 19 September, three separate Confederate assaults in the afternoon almost shatter the Union position. Bragg sends Stewart towards the sound of the firing. Stewart appears on Van Cleve's flank. During a hard-fought hour-long engagement, Stewart drives Van Cleve back across the Lafayette Road. Stewart pursues toward the Widow Glenn's, only to be taken in flank and driven back by Negley's division. Next Hood's two divisions force Davis back and also advance towards the Widow Glenn's. Wilder engages on Johnson's flank. When *Wood and Sheridan reach the field, they attack Hood's flank and drive him back. At dusk, Cleburne, supported by Cheatham, attacks the Federal left. A bitter confused action ensues. Although Cleburne gains ground, he is unable to break Thomas's line.*

been hastening to join their corps around Kelly field. Two fresh Union brigades brushed Stewart's flank and sent the Rebels fleeing back east across the road and into the woods. Stewart's division had fought hard and well but had now shot its bolt. As it retired it encountered the swaggering veterans of the Army of Northern Virginia advancing to the front.

On the afternoon of the previous day a train had chugged and wheezed into Ringgold Station. The doors opened and out came men and horses. A tall man mounted his horse, reins in one hand – his other arm was in a sling – and rode towards Reed's bridge to assume command of an advancing column. It is notable that Bragg had entrusted a 'stranger' from Virginia instead of an

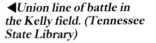

◀*Union line of battle in the Kelly field. (Tennessee State Library)*

◀*Rosecrans and his staff watched the assaults by Stewart and Hood that almost broke the Union centre. (Tennessee State Library)*

Army of Tennessee veteran to execute his offensive. Arriving on the field this rider encountered his old troops for the first time since Gettysburg. They recognized him and offered 'a touching welcome'. It was John Bell Hood and this was his Texas Brigade. At about 4 p.m. next day Hood – now commanding a corps comprising his old division and B. R. Johnson's – pitched into the fray. His line was due west of Alexander's bridge. Hood attacked with his two divisions abreast, Johnson on the left, Law on the right. One of Hood's old veterans called out to Stewart's battered soldiers as he advanced: 'Rise up, Tennesseans, and see the Texans go in!' He spoke with the pride and knowledge that Hood's Texans had shattered many Yankee lines from Gaines Mill to Devil's Den.

The experience of General Jerome Robertson's Texas Brigade typified this second afternoon assault. It had marched a mere 200 yards through the woods when heavy fire from Davis' division opened from the left flank. Hood rode among his men to offer encouragement: 'Move up men, those fellows are shooting in the tops of the trees.' Changing front, the brigade 'steadily advanced, the enemy stubbornly contesting every inch of ground'. Reaching some rising ground, two Union batteries raked Robertson's exposed Texans with grape and canister. Robertson ordered a withdrawal to the reverse slope. Seeing the Texas Brigade recoil, the Union forces counter-attacked. Exhibiting a nice sense of Wellington-like reverse slope tactics, Robertson waited until the Yankees gained the crest and ordered a volley, a cheer, and a charge. His brigade drove the enemy back, but at cost. Here the commanders of the 1st, 4th and 5th Texas Regiments fell wounded. Commanding near the front lines in the only style he knew, Hood too rode amid bullets and shell. His favourite roan, 'Jeff Davis' received a severe wound.

Hood's assault sent the Yankees reeling back west over the Lafayette Road and up the slopes of the Widow Glenn's. A Texan recalls the thrill of pursuit: 'The whole line in front of us seemed broken and confused . . . I was too much excited to notice any except those fleeing in my front. I rushed on, waving my hat, until I was pretty well mixed up with them.' A soldier in the 44th

▲ *According to a participant, hard-fighting Benjamin Franklin Cheatham was '. . . boiling over [with] rage . . . to see his Division driven back* *for the first time in the war'. He received permission to join Cleburne's assault. (Tennessee State Library)*

Alabama wrote that the 'Yankees fought manfully as long as we lay and fought', but once the regiment 'raised a yell, and went at them at a double quick . . . they skedaddled in fine style.' Hood's men became scattered during the wild advance, and this uncovered Johnson's adjacent division on his left. From that direction Wilder's brigade began to tear into the exposed flank. Wilder reported that his brigade and its attached battery delivered '. . . over 200 rounds of double-shotted 10-pound canister, at a range varying from 70 to 350 yards, and at the same time kept up a constant fire with our repeating rifles'. Then Wood's and Sheridan's divisions, the last two of Rosecrans' ten divisions that were to reach the field this day, appeared to join Wilder on the Confederate left. Their advance forced Hood's men to retreat. As the Texas Brigade retired through the ranks of Stewart's men, one soldier could not resist the opportunity: 'Rise up, Tennesseans', he shouted, 'and see the Texans come out!'

The third major Confederate assault of the afternoon involved Cleburne's division. At about 6 p.m. this unit spearheaded a general advance of the Confederate right. Cleburne believed in the value of fast, well-aimed fire and had trained his division relentlessly. When his 5,000 men exploded out of the forest they seemed like double their actual numbers. In near darkness a tremendous fight began, both sides aiming at the flashes of the others' guns: 'In the twilight gloom and smoke . . . the two lines were entangled with each other, and friends could hardly be distinguished from foes.' General Preston Smith rode up to a

Company 'D', 19th Illinois Volunteers, Ellsworth Zouave Cadets, to which this Sergeant belongs, were named after the man who did most to establish the Zouave movement in pre-war America, Ephraim Elmer Ellsworth. Ellsworth was killed on 24 May 1861 whilst removing a Confederate flag from the roof of a Tavern in Alexandria, Virginia, an event which turned him into a national hero. (Shirley Mallinson)

line of men to ask who they were, and was shot and killed when they turned out to be Yankees. Cleburne's attached gunners ran their pieces forward until they were only 60 yards from the enemy line. After about a 30-minute struggle, the defenders fell back, yielding a brace of cannon, several hundred prisoners, and two Colours. More than this Cleburne could not accomplish.

With the exception of Cleburne's attack the day's fighting displayed the pattern of an encounter battle. Two forces met, whomever first received reinforcements overlapped his opponent's flanks and drove him off. Then reinforcements, arriving to support the defeated troops, flanked the charging enemy and drove them, in turn, back on their supports. This process repeated itself throughout the day as the fighting spread north to south. D. H. Hill later described the day's confused, disjointed fight as 'the sparring of the amateur boxer, not the crushing blows of the trained pugilist'. Twice the Confederates penetrated deep into the Union rear, only to become isolated and forced to withdraw for lack of supports. Casualties this day were heavy for both sides. Had the battle ended now, it still would have ranked as one of the major contests of the war. Instead, it was the preamble to an even more desperate engagement.

The night of 19 September was clear and cold, and the wounded suffered. Men searched the field for their comrades while medical service personnel hauled the wounded to field hospitals. As always, the numbers of wounded overwhelmed the medical staff. To keep them warm until they could be dealt with, ambulance train workers arranged them closely in long lines and lit fires near their feet. The Yankees suffered particularly because the main field hospital was at Crawfish Springs, a central position near good water when established, but now on the far fringe of the battle as the army kept sidling to its left. An Alabama soldier recalls building a blazing fire, and although the dead were thick all around, 'yet the men were gay and lively, as full of hope and confident in victory as ever . . . we all felt that we would whip the enemy'.

At about 11 p.m. on 19 September 'Old Rosy' summoned his corps commanders for a conference. Rosecrans enjoyed these discussions; they

▲ *Soon after graduating from West Point in 1827, Leonidas Polk resigned from the US Army in order to study for the ministry. He apparently did no military reading until his friend Jefferson Davis appointed him a major general on the outbreak of the war. He served as a corps commander at Shiloh, Perryville, Murfreesboro and Chickamauga, but his dilatory conduct throughout the Chickamauga campaign angered Bragg. Aged 57, he was much liked and respected by most of his peers, but he was unqualified for the high command Davis thrust upon him, exhibiting neither tactical skill nor any sense of higher strategy. (Tennessee State Library)*

gave him a chance to unwind from the day's tension, and indeed the stress had been high. Not surprisingly, General Phil Sheridan found the general officers 'much depressed' over the day's close calls. Yet the line had held and the army was now concentrated. Rosecrans asked his corps commanders for recommendations. Thomas L. Crittenden had little to say. His great day had come at Murfreesboro where he had won the brevet of brigadier general in the regular army. Characterized as 'a good drinker' and a braggart, he had been promoted beyond his abilities. Alexander McDowell McCook – one of the fighting McCooks of Ohio, seventeen of whom served in the Union army and navy – had led the 1st Ohio at Bull Run before transferring west. He had fought in most of the major battles in Kentucky and Tennessee. At both Perryville and Murfreesboro his command had been routed. Promoted none the less, the 33-year-old McCook too had little to say. Uncharacteristically, it was the Union-loyal Virginian, George Thomas, who was initially

most animated as he reviewed the day's events: 'Whenever I touched their flanks they broke, general, they broke.' Responding to his chief's question about what to do next, Thomas consistently answered, 'I would strengthen the left.' When 'Old Rosy' asked, 'Where are we going to take it from?' there was no answer. Thomas – after two sleepless days and nights of forced marching and a day of hard battle – was asleep, propped upright in his chair. For the remainder of the conference he only stirred to repeat, 'I would

◀ *A Union-loyal Virginian, West Point graduate and Mexican War veteran, George Thomas served during the Army of the Cumberland's early days. He won a fine victory at Mill Springs and then superseded Grant when the latter fell out of favour after Shiloh. He led corps-sized forces at Perryville and Murfreesboro. Aged 45, while nominally commander of XIV Corps at Chickamauga, he in effect served as wing commander. During the conflict's second day, he held the Union left intact after the right had fled the field, thereby earning his sobriquet 'The Rock of Chickamauga'. A huge man, weighing nearly 300 pounds, Thomas's battlefield skills matched his solid physique. His imperturbable nature during crisis and confusion saved the army at Chickamauga. (National Archives)*

strengthen the left.' That is what Rosecrans did. He contracted his front, ordered Thomas to defend in place, ordered McCook to form on Thomas's right, and kept Crittenden with two divisions in reserve. The conference broke up and Thomas returned to his sector at about 2 a.m.

He heard the sound of ringing axes along his front. It came from Union soldiers who were improving their hastily made fence-rail breastworks by cutting logs and clearing fields of fire. He received a report from General Baird, who was defending Thomas's left flank, saying that he lacked the strength to secure it adequately. Thomas inspected the positions by moonlight and concurred. He requested Rosecrans to send Negley's division, which had been sucked into the fight in the Union right-centre, to him. Rosecrans replied that Negley would march at dawn. Reassured, Thomas, like thousands of others, bedded down beneath a large oak, the roots serving as his pillow.

Across the lines, General Braxton Bragg was also preparing for the resumption of the fighting. He appreciated that his forces were 'masters of the ground' after some very difficult fighting. Based on prisoners' reports, he understood that he had faced the entire Union host. He received welcome news that Longstreet had arrived back at the railhead and would reach the field during the evening with two more veteran brigades. Absorbing all this, Bragg summoned his major subordinates to his headquarters. At the meeting was General Hood who, unlike the balky subordinates in the Army of Tennessee, had ridden to headquarters to report 'according to my custom in Virginia under General Lee'. Bragg briefed his subordinates about his plan, which remained unchanged: 'To turn the enemy's left, and by direct atack force him into McLemore's Cove.' He divided his army into two wings, each commanded by his senior lieutenant generals. Polk would begin on the right where he was to attack at dawn, sending his units to the assault in succession from right to left. Longstreet would command the left wing. He would await Polk's attack before beginning his own assault.

A man who enjoyed the comforts of a good life, Polk left the conference and returned to his headquarters at a farmhouse on the southern side of Chickamauga Creek, several miles from his front lines. He left a picket chain with instructions to tell anyone searching for him the whereabouts of his new headquarters, and dispatched couriers to his subordinates to inform them of the planned dawn attack. The courier to Cheatham soon accomplished his mission. Walker, the commander of the Reserve Corps, tracked Polk to his headquarters where he received verbal orders regarding the dawn attack. But then Polk's chain of command broke down. The courier sent to Hill blundered around in the dark forest for four hours and never found him. Hill, in turn, weary from a day in the saddle, rode five miles to Bragg's headquarters, could not find Bragg (because he had relocated) and at about midnight learned from a passing staffer of the new command structure whereby Polk was now his wing commander. He was told that Polk wished to see him, but was three miles distant resting at his farmhouse. Exhibiting a physical and moral collapse, angry at the haphazard command conduct of the Army of Tennessee, annoyed to be subordinated to Polk, Daniel Harvey Hill decided to take a three-hour nap.

Longstreet had reached Bragg's campfires at 11 p.m. He too had expected an escort and guide, but in their absence had found his own way, narrowly avoiding capture when he rode into a Union picket. Bragg awoke to brief him and gave him a crude map. Longstreet understood that his was an important duty, made difficult by his total ignorance of the terrain and lack of familiarity with all his subordinates except the leaders of the five Army of Northern Virginia brigades. Nevertheless, after a few hours rest, he set off to inspect his lines and prepare them for the assault.

Thus the two great rival armies prepared to renew the conflict, each in its own unique way, and together in a haphazard western style so unlike the higher level of professionalism exhibited by the eastern armies. On the Union side Rosecrans had an adequately prepared defence. On the Confederate side Bragg had a sound plan. Where it went awry was with the right wing where those leaders who most heartily detested him were ordered to conduct a dawn assault.

Lull before the Storm: Dispositions about 9 a. m., 20 September

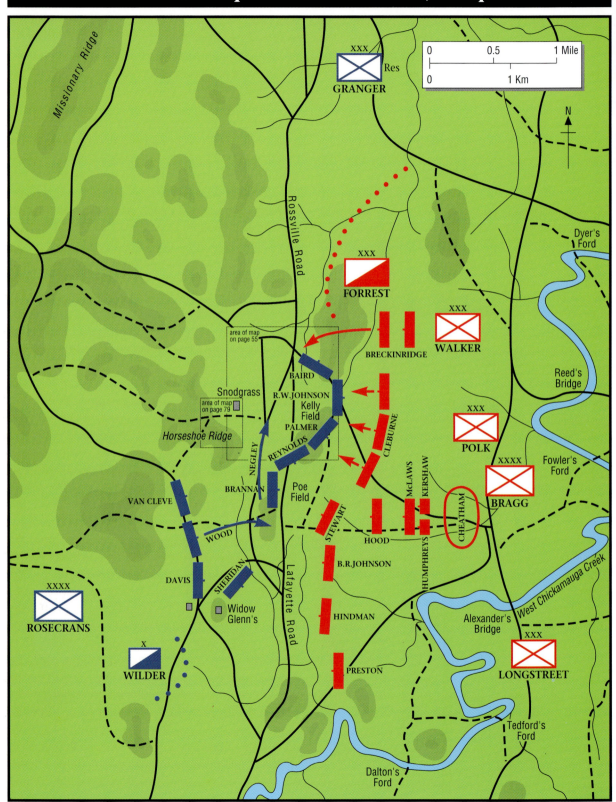

THE SECOND DAY: THE CONFEDERATE RIGHT WING ASSAULT

Sunday morning dawned clear and beautiful. D. H. Hill found his two principal subordinates, Breckinridge and Cleburne, just behind the front on the Confederate right. While they were conversing a courier arrived. Hill reached out to take the orders and the courier told him they were meant for the hands of his two divisional commanders. He explained that when the overnight courier to Hill had returned to Polk's headquarters to report his failed mission, Polk had written directly to Hill's subordinates. Dispatched at 5.30 a.m., Polk's orders read: 'The Lieutenant General commanding having sought in vain for Lieutenant General Hill, gives you directly the following orders: Move upon and attack the enemy so soon as you are in position. Major General Cheatham, on our left, has been ordered to make a simultaneous attack.' Vexed at having to serve under Polk, a fellow lieutenant general, embarrassed in front of his subordinates, Hill found reasons to delay further. The assault brigades were not aligned according to his satisfaction and the men had not yet eaten. He sent word back to Polk that the attack would not begin for another hour or so.

Bragg rose early, rode forward, and at daybreak impatiently awaited Polk's attack. He learned that overnight the Yankees had been felling trees, which prompted him to comment that this activity was all the more reason for the assault to begin immediately. Bragg was right. A Federal officer confirmed that between daylight and the first assault his men 'worked vigorously' building breastworks 'which proved of vast service' during the day. Time passed, the sun rose, and Bragg heard no sounds to indicate that Polk had begun to advance. Finally he sent a staff officer to ascertain the reason for the delay. When the staffer returned without a satisfactory answer, Bragg uttered a terrible oath directed at Polk and Hill and then told his staff to ride along the line and order every captain to take his men into the assault. So, many hours late, and in a disjointed fashion, the Confederate assault along the right began at about 9.30 a.m.

The delay had greatly benefited the men defending Thomas's far left flank. As light penetrated the forest, Brigadier General John King, whose regular brigade was defending this sector, saw that an unprotected open field was skirting his left flank and sent the 1/18 Infantry to occupy a line of timber at the far end of the field to protect it. They had time to carry their log and rail breastworks forward to the new position and settle in before the Rebel assault began, but King remained concerned because there was still a gap separating him from the nearest supporting brigade on his left.

That brigade – John Beatty, Negley's division – had been sent by Rosecrans in response to Thomas's 2 a.m. request. Thomas was expecting the entire division, but someone had blundered, and Negley did not receive the order until 8 a.m. By this time Confederate pressure was building along Negley's front and he could not leave his position until reliefs arrived. Consequently, Beatty arrived late. As Beatty moved to protect King's left

◀ *Bragg has reorganized his army into two wings commanded by Polk and Longstreet. Breckinridge begins approach march to position on Union left flank. Polk's forces are scattered. Walker is available to support Breckinridge, but, with Cheatham, remains in deep reserve. Two brigades of the Army of Northern Virginia, Humphrey's and Kershaw's, have arrived and are in reserve behind Hood. Longstreet has massed his forces in depth and awaits Polk's assault. Rosecrans has made the decision to reinforce Thomas on the Union left to the expense of all else. Command confusion delays Wood's arrival at the front to relieve Negley. Negley, in turn, has not tied into Baird's flank. Granger observes the build-up against Thomas with anxiety.*

he ran into Breckinridge's attacking infantry and was never able to link up with King's flank.

Breckinridge's division had been involved in only light skirmishing on the previous day. Transferred to the Confederate right flank during the night, Breckinridge had to deploy his 3,769 men without any knowledge of the terrain. When finally released by Hill at 9.30 a.m., Breckinridge's three brigades still had little idea of the whereabouts of the Federal line. No officer in the division seems to have usefully employed the time for a reconnais-sance. The divisional line ran: from right to left Adams, Stovall and Helm. All Stovall's and Adams' men and part of Helm's brigade over-lapped the Union breastworks. Initially they advanced into thin air. Meanwhile 2nd and 9th Kentucky, and three companies of 42nd Alabama on Helm's left encountered King's defended breastworks. Breckinridge called Helm's unit his 'Orphan Brigade' because all except one regiment hailed from Kentucky and, ever since Bragg's failed invasion of 1862, had been orphaned from

▶ *A Union soldier described receiving a Confederate attack at Chickamauga: 'Then the firing broke out again . . . first the scattering fire of skirmishers – then the terrific file firing of regiments, then the artillery, then the Rebel yell, and the firing gradually approached us.' (Library of Congress)*

▶ *General Ben Hardin Helm – who had married Mary Lincoln's youngest sister – fell mortally wounded in front of the breastworks. (Tennessee State Library)*

◀ *A Kentucky-born politician, John Breckinridge enjoyed a fast rise culminating in his successful candidacy for the Vice-Presidency of the United States in 1856. Appointed a Confederate brigadier for political reasons in 1861, he rose to major general and commanded the Reserve Corps at Shiloh. He led a division at Murfreesboro and at Chickamauga. An enthusiastic amateur, he was a better politician than general, and an even better drinker. (National Archives)*

their home state. Breckinridge, a Kentuckian himself, expected much from his orphans and they tried to oblige.

They charged into a terrible mix of rifle fire from the works in front and rifle and cannon fire enfilading their line from the left. Bragg's plan called for a sequential assault which meant that

there was no Confederate pressure initially applied against the men manning the breastworks to Helm's left. So these defenders were free to concentrate their fire against the men of the Orphan Brigade. One defending regiment, the 29th Indiana, described pouring 'a galling fire' into the Orphan Brigade at ranges of 100 to 150 yards as it advanced against the regulars. The Federal line was on the crest of a low ridge with a cleared area some 75 yards deep extending in front of the works. This clearing offered a perfect killing ground. A Rebel soldier described the scene: 'Thud! and down goes Private Robertson. He turned, smiled and died. Thud! Corporal Gray shot through the neck. "Get to the rear!" said I. Thud! Thud! Thud! and three more fall. The pressure is fearful.' The Confederates advanced with great gallantry. The colour-bearers led the way, carrying their Hardee-style banners – blue field with large white ball in the centre – close to the defenders' works. The colour sergeant of the 2nd Kentucky managed to plant his standard on the works before being shot and killed. Here the colonel of 4th Kentucky received a wound while the colonel of 2nd Kentucky and General Helm both died. Repulsed, they reformed and charged again only to be shot back after reaching a point some 40 yards from the fire-tinged breastworks.

▶ *Breckinridge initiates Bragg's offensive on the morning of 20 September. Adams, Stovall and elements of Helm overlap King's flank. While 2nd and 9th Kentucky, and elements of 41st Alabama attack King's works, the balance of the division drive J. Beatty and achieve a position in Thomas's rear. After changing front, Stovall and Adams advance only to be hit in flank by Stanley and from the front by Van Derveer. Had Breckinridge's attack been properly supported, Thomas's position would have collapsed.*

▲ *Breckinridge's attack against Thomas's left. The spacing from monument to monument is a Confederate regimental front.*

While Helm's men were dying in front of King's position, the balance of Breckinridge's division continued through the forest until they ran into John Beatty's brigade. These Yankees offered but a feeble resistance. A captain in the 42nd Indiana ran to a regiment of advancing Georgians to surrender both himself and his entire company, explaining that they had been in Beatty's picket line but the Rebel advance had cut them off. A Louisiana colonel reported, 'We fell upon [Beatty] with such impetuosity that he broke in confusion, the men throwing away their arms and equipment.' Bridges' Battery of Illinois Light Artillery briefly checked the advance, but the Confederates worked through the woods to a flank position and shot down horses and gunners alike. Bridges ordered a retreat but Rebel marksmen killed the senior lieutenant of the tardiest two-gun section while he was supervising the withdrawal. Their fire downed the still standing battery horses including the one Bridges himself rode. Storming ahead, the Confederates captured two guns while the rest of the battery cantered to the rear. Spearheaded by the 14th Louisiana sharpshooter battalion, Adams' brigade on the Confederate right cut the road leading from Thomas's rear back through McFarland's Gap. Breckinridge assessed the situation: 'It

was now evident, from the comparatively slight resistance they had encountered and the fact that they were not threatened in front, that our line had extended beyond the enemy's left. I at once ordered these brigades to change front ... to advance upon the flank of the enemy.'

The Confederate attack placed King's regulars in a perilous situation. They saw a large number of John Beatty's broken men stream into the field behind their line just before elements of Breckinridge's column turned to pour a terrible enfilade fire into them. Breckinridge's fire forced the nearest units to fold back at right angles to the original line. Here Bugler Carson, who the day before had rallied the brigade with his inspired conduct, took up a musket, nominated himself as provost guard and prevented anyone from retreating. It also helped a great deal that the divisional commander, Absalom Baird, was keeping cool in the midst of crisis.

Seeing King's men falling back, it appeared to Baird that 'our line seemed ready to crumble'. He ordered his second line to stand and change front to face the Rebels. The second line comprised troops from several different commands, and this made the manoeuvre more difficult. Seeing them waver, Baird rode to the front of two regiments from his own division and ordered them to charge. His men greeted Baird with a cheer and charged toward the south-west. By happy good fortune – and good leadership, Thomas directing them to

Breckinridge's Assault, 9.30 a. m., 20 September

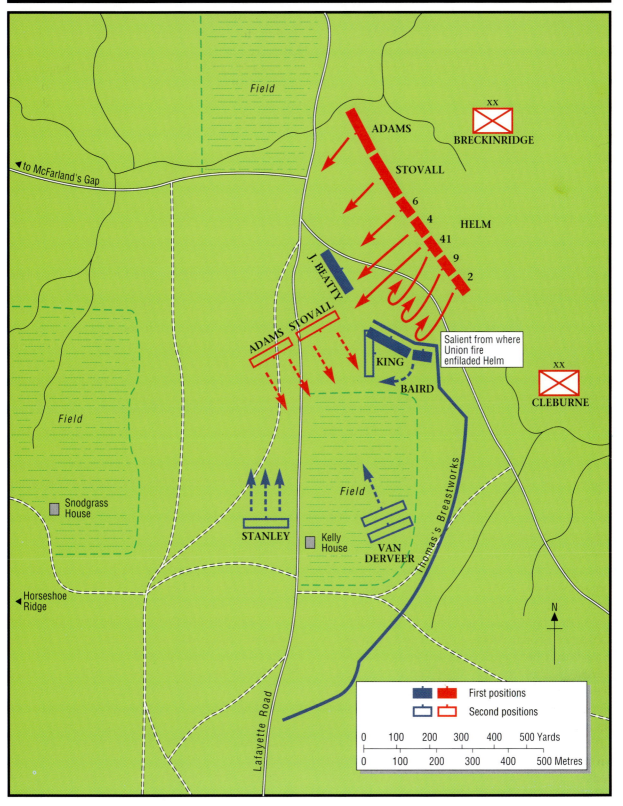

Field

to McFarland's Gap ◄

XX

BRECKINRIDGE

ADAMS

STOVALL

6

4   HELM

41

9

2

J. BEATTY

ADAMS STOVALL

Salient from where
Union fire
enfiladed Helm

KING

BAIRD

XX

CLEBURNE

Field

Snodgrass
House

Field

STANLEY

Kelly
House

VAN
DERVEER

Thomas's Breastworks

Horseshoe
Ridge ◄

N

Lafayette Road

		First positions
		Second positions

0	100	200	300	400	500 Yards
0	100	200	300	400	500 Metres

the point where they were most needed – almost simultaneously Colonel Stanley, commanding the second of Negley's brigades, appeared from the south to place Breckinridge in a deadly vice.

The conflict raged fiercely. Brigadier General Stovall reported, 'A concentrated fire of grape and canister, shot and shell of every conceivable character, was poured into us.' Stovall's men struggled forward; the colour-bearer of the 3rd Florida Infantry fell less than a dozen paces from the Federal line. Then fire from the south, indicating the arrival of yet another fresh Union force, hit the Rebel right flank. This fire came from Colonel Van Derveer's brigade which had been in reserve until Breckinridge's attack exploded beyond the Federal flank. Thomas ordered Van Derveer to go to Baird's support. Marching into the Kelly field, Van Derveer saw four distinct enemy lines charging toward the Union rear. The colonel wheeled his line to block the charge and ordered his men to lie down. When Stovall's brigade had approached to within 75 yards, Van Derveer's front two regiments sprang up and delivered a volley. The rear two regiments passed the lines, fired, and the entire Yankee brigade charged, driving the Confederates before them.

Confederate brigade order collapsed as individual regiments drifted out of line, which gave each regiment the impression that it was fighting alone. Most of the regimental leaders later complained of severe enfilade fire caused by the lack of flank supports. While Van Derveer and King dealt with Stovall, Stanley's brigade – assisted by some of John Beatty's rallied men – struck Adams' brigade. A soldier in the 19th Illinois recalls his regiment rising to their knees, firing a volley at 30 paces, and charging. The Rebels had not seen them until hit by pointblank fire. Here the unlucky Brigadier Daniel Adams, who had lost an eye at Shiloh and been severely wounded at Murfreesboro, was shot from his horse and captured. The loss of key brigade and regimental officers just as the assault was in full career impaired coordination and caused the Rebel advance to pause as staff officers desperately searched for the senior survivor so that they could deliver orders, and men looked for replacements for their fallen commanders. Breckinridge's division had made a game

try; about one in three was hit during the morning assault. Slowly, after more than an hour-long struggle, Breckinridge's survivors fell back thereby ending, for the moment, the threat to Thomas's left flank.

Shortly after Breckinridge had begun his assault, Hill passed the word to Cleburne to dress on Breckinridge and go in. The ground Cleburne's division had to traverse ran slightly uphill through open woods. Three Union divisions, representing three different corps, occupied the breastworks facing Cleburne. Each division had at least one-third of its strength in reserve. To fight the eight defending brigades, Cleburne arranged his three brigades in a long line and led with the rightmost brigade, commanded by brigadier general Lucius Polk, a nephew of the wing commander. The attackers had little idea about the dispositions of the opposing line of breastworks until the defenders opened fire. Polk reported, 'My line from right to left soon became furiously engaged, the enemy pouring a most destructive fire of canister and musketry into my advancing line – so terrible, indeed, that my line could not advance in the face of it, but lying down continued the fight for another hour and one half.'

Continuing the echelon attack, Deshler's brigade advanced next followed by Wood, who went in on Cleburne's far left shortly after 10 a.m. Elements of the two brigades entered a clearing that ran between 200 and 500 yards from the Union works. Here the defenders spied them and opened fire. Patrick Cleburne had seen much of war and, unlike many officers, wrote his reports with studied understatement. Yet he described this fire as 'the heaviest I ever heard'. In the middle of the clearing was a gentle swale which provided a little shelter from the terrible fire. Here the attackers went to ground, the long-range Federal fire preventing them from advancing any farther. The Rebels fired back, aware that it was a most unequal contest since their targets were concealed behind their works. A Mississippi colonel reported that the only target his regiment could see was the smoke from a Yankee battery some 230 yards ahead.

Behind the Confederate lines there were few stragglers but 'a continual stream' of wounded flowing to the field hospitals, '... the wounded infantryman crutching it along on his gun, and the mangled artilleryman clinging to his bleeding and staggering battery horse'. They were too stubborn to yield until, after more than an hour of suffering, Cleburne ordered a withdrawal. In total, Cleburne's division lost about 1,300 men during an assault that never got to within 100 yards of the Federal works, and typically went to ground more than 200 yards away. Yet their stubborn persistence accomplished something important; they thoroughly engaged the attention of R. W. Johnson's, Palmer's and Reynolds' divisions.

With Breckinridge repulsed and Cleburne stalled, General D. H. Hill cast about for reinforcements to get his advance moving again. Since daylight Walker's Reserve Corps had been standing idle. At about 10 a.m. Hill asked Walker for a loan of a brigade, refused the one nearest, and remarked that only Gist's brigade would do. The 32-year-old States Rights Gist – a South Carolinian born, ironically, in Union District – was one of those red hot secessionists that South Carolina bred in such abundance. A graduate of Harvard law school, Gist's previous combat experience had been limited. His brigade was part of the force sent from Mississippi to reinforce Bragg. The brigade's 980 men reached Bragg's railhead on the 19th and did not arrive at the battlefield in time to participate in the first day's action. In the crazy quilt Confederate command structure, Walker had only minutes before placed Gist in command of the division. This probably saved Gist's life, for it was the senior colonel, Peyton Colquitt, who now led the brigade forward.

It advanced along the same line followed earlier in the morning by Helm. There was no effort to learn about the Yankee line from any of Helm's officers, so Colquitt had no idea where the enemy was and drifted too far to his right when the defenders, King's regulars again, opened fire. Only the 24th South Carolina actually faced King's works, the balance of the brigade flank marching past. Thus they repeated Helm's experience and confronted 'a severe and destructive enfilading fire'. The attack collapsed, more than a third of the brigade was hit, only two field officers remained standing, and Colquitt fell dead, the

▲*Thomas's defending divisions faced such furious 'assault after assault' from Patrick Cleburne's troops that he was reluctant to weaken the line by withdrawing men to reinforce other threatened sectors. (Tennessee State Library)*

third Confederate brigade commander killed during the morning assaults against Thomas's works. Colquitt's charge had been an uncoordinated bungle.

Longstreet's Assault

Unlike the indolent Polk, newly arrived James B. Longstreet had displayed great energy during the night, and it showed. After receiving instructions from Bragg at 11 p.m., he met as many of his subordinates as he could and then at daybreak rode forward to deploy his forces. He encountered Hood and questioned him about the formation of the lines, the men's spirits and the effect the Confederate attacks had had upon the Yankees.

◄ The 43-year-old James Longstreet's brilliant tactical leadership was instrumental in winning the battle of Chickamauga. A western soldier viewing him on the battlefield wrote, 'Longstreet is the boldest and bravest-looking man I ever saw. I don't think he would dodge if a shell were to burst under his chin.' (National Archives)

Hood replied that the officers and men were in fine fettle, they had driven the enemy fully one mile the previous day, and would rout him this day. Longstreet replied that '. . . we would of course whip and drive him from the field.' Hood expressed his delight that Longstreet 'was the first general I had met since my arrival who talked of victory'.

Also in contrast to other generals, and particularly compared to the Confederate right wing, Longstreet so deployed his wing as to pack a concentrated punch. Longstreet massed his seventeen brigades along a front that extended a mere one and a quarter miles. His rightmost division, commanded by Stewart, linked his wing with Polk's wing and stood adjacent to Cleburne's division. Next in line came Johnson, Hindman, and Preston. To achieve even more massed striking power, Longstreet ordered all divisions of three brigades to have two brigades in the front line and one in reserve. Larger divisions had two brigades in reserve. Moreover, Hood's three brigades massed in column behind Johnson while Kershaw's and Humphreys' newly arrived Virginia veterans deployed in a fourth line behind them. Then Longstreet waited for Polk's attack to begin.

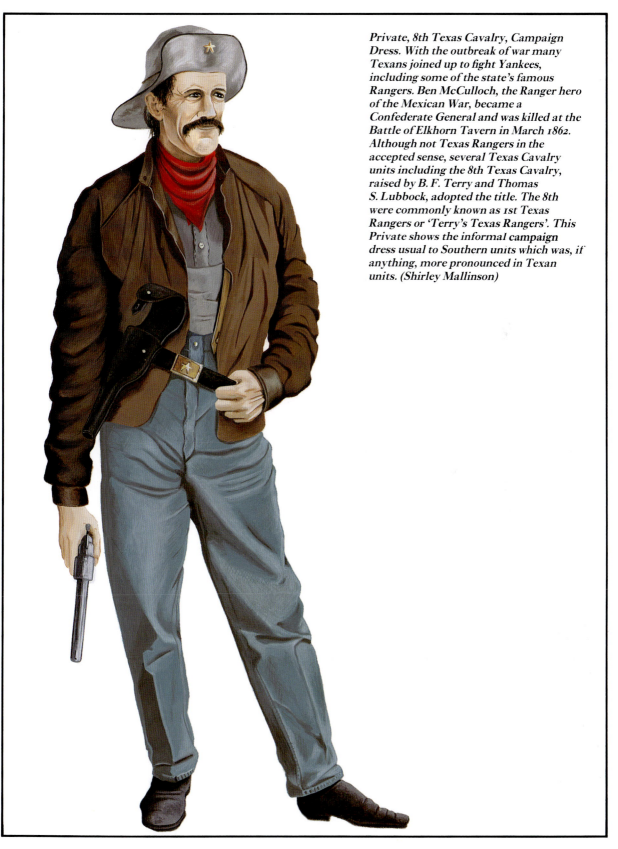

Private, 8th Texas Cavalry, Campaign Dress. With the outbreak of war many Texans joined up to fight Yankees, including some of the state's famous Rangers. Ben McCulloch, the Ranger hero of the Mexican War, became a Confederate General and was killed at the Battle of Elkhorn Tavern in March 1862. Although not Texas Rangers in the accepted sense, several Texas Cavalry units including the 8th Texas Cavalry, raised by B. F. Terry and Thomas S. Lubbock, adopted the title. The 8th were commonly known as 1st Texas Rangers or 'Terry's Texas Rangers'. This Private shows the informal campaign dress usual to Southern units which was, if anything, more pronounced in Texan units. (Shirley Mallinson)

The early morning's silence puzzled him as it did everyone from Bragg down. At last, at about 9.30 the roar of battle began on the far right with great fury. But, as he later reported, 'it did not progress as had been anticipated'. As we have seen, this stemmed from the considerable command confusion that haunted Polk's wing, but Longstreet did not know this. Showing commendable initiative of exactly the sort that had been so lacking on the second day at Gettysburg, Longstreet sent a messenger to Bragg suggesting that he begin his attack. His courier passed one of Bragg's who conveyed orders to attack. However, as had been the case with Polk's wing, Bragg's staffers – obeying their chief's directives to order every captain to lead his men to the attack – had carried the attack order directly to Longstreet's subordinates. Thus Stewart began to advance before Longstreet knew about Bragg's order. This impatient improvisation almost undid Longstreet's careful preparations since it caused the attack to begin piecemeal. Vexed, Longstreet quickly perfected his alignments and ordered the whole of his command forward except Preston, whom he retained as a reserve and to protect his left flank.

During the ten minutes or so that Longstreet required before advancing, Stewart responded to Bragg's orders and charged with two brigades up – Bate on the right, Brown on the left – and Clayton in reserve. They entered a maelstrom of shot, shell and Minié ball fired by defenders comfortably hidden behind their breastworks. Exposed to a heavy enfilade fire pouring into their right flank, several of Bate's regiments broke. The problem here was that Thomas's line formed a shallow salient and began angling west back towards the Union rear at a position approximately opposite Stewart's line of departure. The woods obscured this fact from the Confederates until men began to fall from the enfilade fire.

Bate's remnant charged to within 40 paces of the Union line before being repulsed. Three out of every ten men who began the charge were hit and the brigadier himself had two horses shot from under him. Meanwhile Brown's command, the other lead brigade, continued forward towards the Lafayette Road. Here it overran a first line of works, received a punishing enfilade fire from a Union battery positioned on the road itself, and pressed on another several hundred yards before encountering a second line of Union works. By now Bate had been repulsed so Brown faced fire from front and right. Although the reserve brigade joined the assault, it contributed nothing except more casualties. The Federal fire proved too much and the two brigades sullenly retired. In sum, Stewart's division shared the fate of Polk's command who assaulted the Union works. They exhibited great valour, suffered fearful losses, and were repulsed.

About ten minutes after Stewart began his advance the balance of Longstreet's wing moved forward. Longstreet correctly perceived that the failure of any division on his right to break the Union line meant that Bragg's battle plan was no longer workable. Therefore, instead of pivoting his wing to the left, he reversed Bragg's plan by pivoting to the right on the anchor provided by Stewart's division. It was their great good fortune that at the moment Longstreet's men advanced, the opposing defenders were involved in a complicated flank march that left them hugely vulnerable.

Only forty minutes earlier, at 10.30 a.m., the Union troops confronting Longstreet's wing had been in good order, but the steady pressure against the Yankee left forced Thomas to keep requesting reinforcements. Rosecrans obliged by withdrawing various brigades from McCook and Crittenden and sending them on a flank march to Thomas. Each time this occurred the remaining Federal forces had to sidle to their left to fill the gap created by the departing unit. At best, these marches and manoeuvres would have left the defenders unbraced for an attack. What actually transpired was much worse. Minutes before Longstreet's blow landed, an incredible command mixup occurred that left a hole two brigade widths wide at precisely the point where Longstreet had concentrated his assault column.

At 10.45 a certain Captain Kellog, an aide-de-camp to Thomas, appeared at Rosecrans' headquarters. Kellog had just coursed the field behind the Union line and had troubling news. He told Rosecrans that Brannon 'was out of line' and this left Reynolds' right flank exposed and vulnerable. Until now Rosecrans had managed to retain control. He had made the decision that Thomas's position 'must be held at all hazards' even if the entire Union right had to abandon its positions and shift toward Thomas. He had notified McCook of this decision and then worked to hurry reinforcements to the hard-pressed Thomas. Kellog's report changed everything. Alarmed, Rosecrans reacted quickly. Up to now his chief of staff, General James Garfield, had marked current positions on a map using pins. Since most manoeuvres took place in jumbled, wooded terrain, it was extremely difficult for even Garfield to keep track of who was where. But when Kellog appeared Garfield was 'deeply engaged in another matter' so the duty of order writing devolved upon a major who was less familiar with the situation. Like Rosecrans, he accepted the report as true, translated Old Rosy's intentions into a written order, and sent a courier at the gallop to rectify the situation.

At 10.55 the hard-riding courier reined in before General Wood and handed him a dispatch which read: 'The general commanding directs that you close up on Reynolds as fast as possible, and support him.' Wood considered. His division stood adjacent to Brannon's division while Reynolds, in turn, was next in line toward the left. To obey required that he pull out of line and march across Brannon's rear. Even while Wood pondered, skirmishers – Bushrod Johnson's men – were beginning to engage a mere 300 yards in front of his position. However, fresh in Wood's mind was an unpleasant experience that had taken place about an hour previously.

At that time several Federal brigades had become intermingled during the complicated manoeuvres required to send Negley to Thomas. Rosecrans, who had been receiving regular and increasingly frequent appeals from Thomas for reinforcements, lost his temper and sought out the culprit. He landed upon Wood and upbraided him publicly: 'By your damnable negligence you are endangering the safety of the entire army, and by God I will not tolerate it! Move your division at once, as I have instructed, or the consequences will not be pleasant for yourself.' Wood, an experienced veteran and a West Pointer, had swallowed his anger and obeyed.

Now, Wood had new orders that made little sense but had been sent directly from his commanding general. General McCook happened to be with Wood when the order arrived. Although McCook did not command the corps to which Wood belonged, Wood consulted him briefly. Still smarting from his recent dressing-down regarding his slowness to obey orders, Wood withdrew his division from the line. McCook approved of this and promised to direct Davis to fill the gap. As his men began to move Wood rode ahead to scout. Encountering Thomas, he described his orders and asked where he should position his brigades. Thomas replied that Reynolds did not need any assistance – Reynolds and Brannon had just successfully repulsed Stewart – but that Baird at the far end of the line urgently needed help. This was all a puzzle, the dimensions of which only became clear to Wood later. For the present he rode back to his division to direct it to Baird's support.

This then was the position of the Army of the Cumberland's right wing shortly after 11 a.m. In a mistaken effort to fill a gap that did not exist, a gap had been created. From left to right and behind the front line with their right flanks facing the Confederate battleline were: Van Cleve's division temporarily at rest behind Brannon; two of Wood's brigades pulling out of line and forming for a flank march to the left; two of Sheridan's brigades filing to the left en route for Thomas's lines. All that remained in the front line were two of Davis' much reduced brigades, some 1,300 men. One of these manned breastworks on what had been Wood's right, the other was in motion toward the position Wood had vacated. An interval of two brigades separated Davis' right from the nearest support, Wilder, while an even wider gap intervened between Davis and Brannon. The only immediately available reserve was Laibolt, of Sheridan's division, who was moving toward Davis' right. At this point the Rebels struck.

Bushrod Johnson's division charged toward the Brotherton farm and achieved a clean breakthrough. McNair, commanding the rightmost brigade, had the good fortune to hit directly into the gap caused by Wood's departure. It advanced three-quarters of a mile until stopped by a

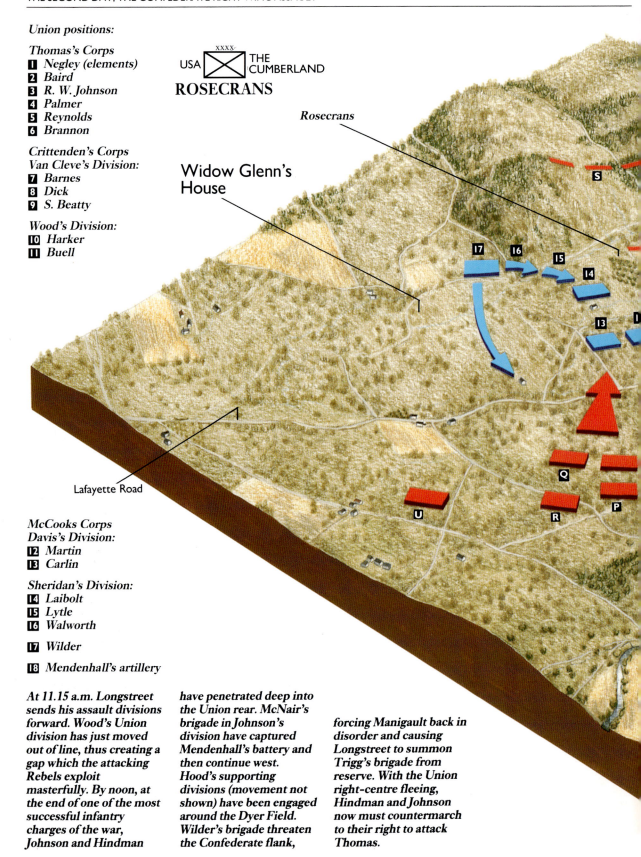

Union positions:

Thomas's Corps
1 Negley (elements)
2 Baird
3 R. W. Johnson
4 Palmer
5 Reynolds
6 Brannon

Crittenden's Corps
Van Cleve's Division:
7 Barnes
8 Dick
9 S. Beatty

Wood's Division:
10 Harker
11 Buell

USA XXXX THE CUMBERLAND
ROSECRANS

Rosecrans

Widow Glenn's House

Lafayette Road

McCooks Corps
Davis's Division:
12 Martin
13 Carlin

Sheridan's Division:
14 Laibolt
15 Lytle
16 Walworth

17 Wilder

18 Mendenhall's artillery

At 11.15 a.m. Longstreet sends his assault divisions forward. Wood's Union division has just moved out of line, thus creating a gap which the attacking Rebels exploit masterfully. By noon, at the end of one of the most successful infantry charges of the war, Johnson and Hindman have penetrated deep into the Union rear. McNair's brigade in Johnson's division have captured Mendenhall's battery and then continue west. Hood's supporting divisions (movement not shown) have been engaged around the Dyer Field. Wilder's brigade threaten the Confederate flank, forcing Manigault back in disorder and causing Longstreet to summon Trigg's brigade from reserve. With the Union right-centre fleeing, Hindman and Johnson now must countermarch to their right to attack Thomas.

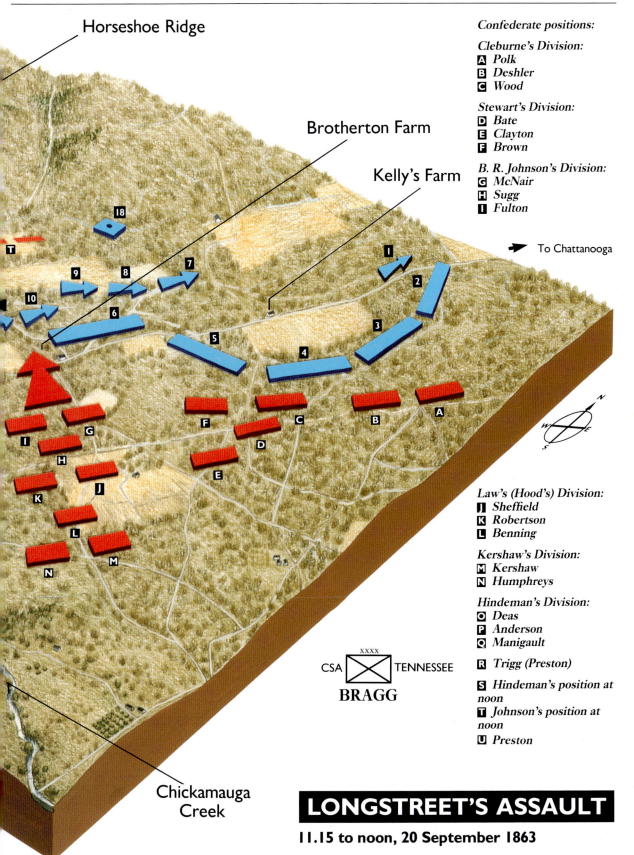

Horseshoe Ridge

Brotherton Farm

Kelly's Farm

Confederate positions:

Cleburne's Division:
A *Polk*
B *Deshler*
C *Wood*

Stewart's Division:
D *Bate*
E *Clayton*
F *Brown*

B. R. Johnson's Division:
G *McNair*
H *Sugg*
I *Fulton*

To Chattanooga

Law's (Hood's) Division:
J *Sheffield*
K *Robertson*
L *Benning*

Kershaw's Division:
M *Kershaw*
N *Humphreys*

Hindeman's Division:
O *Deas*
P *Anderson*
Q *Manigault*

R *Trigg (Preston)*

S *Hindeman's position at noon*

T *Johnson's position at noon*

U *Preston*

xxxx
CSA ⊠ TENNESSEE
BRAGG

Chickamauga Creek

LONGSTREET'S ASSAULT

11.15 to noon, 20 September 1863

▲ Bushrod Johnson's division spearheaded one of the most successful assaults of the war. (US Army Military History Institute)

▲ Advancing adjacent to Johnson was Thomas Hindman's division. As his 22nd Alabama pushed forward, 'The enemy's shot . . . struck us thicker and faster . . . this excited us and we were not allowed to return the fire, we advanced faster, I shot one man down within ten paces of me with his gun pointed at me.' (Tennessee State Library)

formidable Union artillery position firing across the Dyer field from a commanding elevation. McNair and the colonel of the 1st Arkansas (dismounted) Rifles fell here, but the senior surviving officer rallied the command and ordered a charge toward the guns.

Meanwhile Bushrod Johnson's left brigade swept through the Brotherton farmyard where it caught the 100th Illinois in motion to the flank, captured its colonel and a score of its men and, supported by Everett's battery, swept on. The brief check around the Brotherton farm allowed first the reserve brigade and then Hood's men to catch up. Somewhat intermingled, the entire host continued through thick woodland until they emerged on to open ground. Here they could see the Yankees fleeing under cover of the batteries that had

stopped McNair, as well as another battery firing from the left flank. Bushrod Johnson described the scene: 'The resolute and impetuous charge, the rush of our heavy columns sweeping out from the shadow and gloom of the forest into the open fields flooded with sunlight, the glitter of arms, the onward dash of artillery and mounted men, the retreat of the foe, the shouts of the hosts of our army, the dust, the smoke, the noise of firearms – of whistling balls and grape-shot and of bursting shell – made up a battle scene of unsurpassed grandeur. Here General Hood gave me the last order I received from him on the field, "Go ahead, and keep ahead of everything."' Johnson's men met Hood's expectations. The reserve brigade passed McNair's line, wheeled right and prepared to charge across the Dyer field towards the Union

▲ *The Brotherton farm. Hindman's men came out of the woods to the cabin's right and in this farmyard encountered the 100th Illinois. Later these guns of Bledsoe's Missouri*

Battery supported the Confederate breakthrough.

batteries. These guns were present thanks to the exertions of XXI Corps' chief of artillery, Major John Mendenhall.

Mendenhall had assembled 26 guns from five batteries on a spur of Missionary Ridge overlooking the Dyer field. Their position was risky, lacking infantry support to control the adjacent woods. Worse, the fleeing Federal infantry were badly obstructing their field of fire. An officer with the guns looked over the Dyer field and saw the attackers crowding through the corn in heavy column. His description captures the tension: 'The number of stragglers or disorganized troops passing our position, and the confusion existing among our ammunition wagons, and the continuous roar of the artillery and musketry, indicated that the right and center were being driven.'

The gunners themselves were shaky, several batteries having already narrowly avoided being overrun during the initial Confederate push. Now, hastily assembled – one battery reached the position simultaneously with the Rebel charge – they looked down to see their foe advancing 'in splendid style in heavy lines'. Some Rebel marksmen worked around the woods to Mendenhall's rear and began shooting down the gunners, some of whom, without orders, began limbering their pieces to take them to the rear. Others fought hard. The 26th Pennsylvania Battery fired all its canister before trying to limber and withdraw. But it was too late. The Rebels shot down the battery's horses and the brush was too thick for the gunners to drag the guns out. The Confederates would later dispute which brigade captured how many guns, but together, McNair and Johnson with support from Law, captured fifteen pieces of artillery and sent the remainder fleeing back through the pass on Missionary Ridge.

Johnson's division continued west to another rise 600 yards deeper within the Union position. From this elevation they could see the telegraph

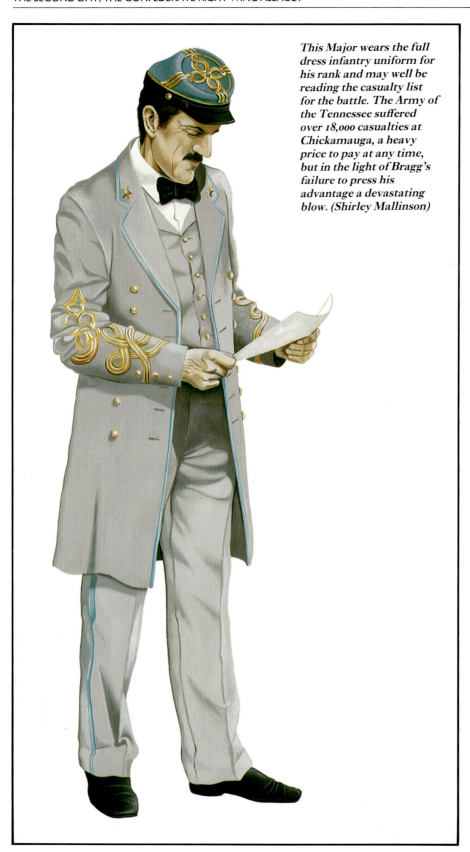

This Major wears the full dress infantry uniform for his rank and may well be reading the casualty list for the battle. The Army of the Tennessee suffered over 18,000 casualties at Chickamauga, a heavy price to pay at any time, but in the light of Bragg's failure to press his advantage a devastating blow. (Shirley Mallinson)

▶ Martin's brigade in Davis' division manned a breastworks overlooking this field. Elements of Deas' brigade charged out of the woods toward the gun in the foreground. A desperate 20-minute engagement ensued during which the 22nd Alabama lost its third colour-bearer and its colonel.

line running from Rosecrans' headquarters back through McFarland's Gap and on to Chattanooga. Through this gap fled the defeated men of Wood's, Davis' and Sheridan's forces. They also could see that they were quite alone, having diverged from Hindman's division on the left and Hood's on the right. It was close to noon, a forty-minute advance now ended. Johnson set his artillery to bombarding the panic-stricken Yankees and rode back to find support.

He traversed a scene of considerable confusion. The Confederate penetration of the Union position was narrow. The units flanking the breakthrough still showed fight and Union artillery dominated the fields to Johnson's rear. Johnson saw that the Federals had re-occupied the artillery position where his men had captured the guns earlier in their charge. Finally, he encountered Hindman and learned what had transpired on his front.

Advancing simultaneously with Johnson, Hindman's fresh division – its three brigades had not engaged on the 19th – had enjoyed great success. Deas' brigade on Hindman's right had shared the good fortune of Johnson's division by attacking through the void left by Wood's departure. Only two of Deas' six attacking units had

confronted defended breastworks. The 19th Alabama had absorbed a pointblank volley, faltered momentarily, and then charged over the Union works. The regiment had taken heavy losses including two colour-bearers, but the rest of the brigade had clambered over undefended breastworks with little difficulty, scooping up prisoners by the handful. Just behind the works they had seen a Yankee column facing north, its flank and rear unprotected.

This was Buell's brigade. When Wood ordered Colonel Buell out of the line the colonel believed it to be a terrible mistake. Buell rode to Davis to warn him that orders required Buell to depart. Having alerted the neighbouring command, the colonel returned to supervise the flank march. Because the Rebels were only 200 yards in front of his brigade, he left his skirmish line in place as a screen. The balance of his command was in motion parallel with the gap left by the withdrawal of the preceding brigade 'when the shock came like an avalanche on my right flank'. Only the regiment in the van and the accompanying battery escaped the blow, the remainder being routed.

Some 200 yards farther along, the leftmost elements of Deas' brigade encountered a second line of works partially manned by Martin's brigade,

in Davis' division. Alerted by Davis that there was a gap in the line to be filled, Martin had just hustled his men into position 'when the enemy rose up from the tall weeds in front and advanced on us four columns deep, pouring in a destructive fire'. The Confederates facing the breastworks were unable to advance until support from the reserve brigade arrived. These supports turned the Federal left flank. The defenders resisted until the Rebels reached the top of their breastworks. Then, 'outflanked, exposed to a raking cross-fire and almost surrounded', Martin's brigade tried to withdraw. It did so with skill and courage, leaving behind only 107 men, many of whom were wounded and unable to move. But having escaped, the brigade was broken up during its retreat through the woods.

While this fight was taking place the remainder of Deas' brigade went on to strike the flank of yet another Union formation, this time Sheridan's division. Manoeuvring behind the position abandoned by Wood, Walworth's brigade was strung out in column in the woods when Deas' Rebels erupted with no warning on its exposed right flank. Walworth immediately ordered the regiment in the van, the 22nd Illinois, to face the enemy and deploy. But the charging Rebels swamped the regiment on both flanks, driving it and most of the brigade to the rear. Only the 27th Illinois, the brigade's rearmost unit, escaped the débâcle. Deploying under heavy fire near the Widow Glenn's, supported by three field pieces of the 1st Missouri Light Artillery, the 27th repulsed Deas' first charge.

Marching behind Walworth came Lytle's Brigade. Led by its inspiring commander, the brigade managed to deploy at the double under heavy fire. Already wounded two or three times, Lytle fell dead from his horse as the Rebels closed in against his brigade's front and both flanks. The 21st Michigan lay down while fleeing bluecoats passed over their line and then rose to deliver a withering volley which checked the first charge. A large party of Rebels worked around the regiment's right flank only to be driven back by the rapid fire of Company 'A' whose men were armed with the Colt revolving rifle. Fresh Confederate troops appeared – Hindman's reserve brigade led by Patton Ander-

son – and after a 20-minute fight the entire brigade yielded.

Meanwhile Hindman's other front-line brigade, South Carolina and Alabama regiments commanded by Manigault, '. . . found themselves within 90 or 100 yards of the enemy's line of battle, their men screened and lying down behind a rough breastworks of logs. Instantly a fringe of smoke rose above their works and a terrific fire assailed [our men], crashing through their ranks, and laying low many a fellow . . . The order to charge was given, but altho no one turned to retreat, it was impossible to make them advance. The only thing to do was to return the fire.' The defenders, Carlin's brigade in Davis' division, were sensitive to the deep penetration of their rear by Deas' brigade. Those nearest the penetration wavered, which induced Manigault's men to charge. Before contact the defenders broke, abandoning three artillery pieces. But the fire fight along this line caused Manigault's men to lose contact with Deas. Alarmed at his isolation, Manigault grew even more anxious when a brisk enfilade fire began pouring into his left flank. It was coming from Wilder's Lightning Brigade.

Wilder's men had spent the morning protecting Rosecrans' right flank. When Wilder saw Longstreet's attack overwhelm Sheridan's division, he ordered his lead regiment, the 98th Illinois, to change front to the left and charge at the double. The 98th's charge bore in against the Widow Glenn's house where Manigault had just overrun a Union battery. Joining them, thanks to the initiative of a Union staff officer, was the 39th Indiana, another Spencer-armed regiment of mounted infantry that had been picketing the army's right flank. Dismounting, firing fast, led by the 98th's colonel, they recaptured the battery. The remainder of the brigade came up and together Wilder's men continued to charge against the Rebel flank. The brigade's attached battery supported the charge by firing canister and shell into Manigault's ranks. A soldier in the 39th Indiana recalled the scene: 'At a distance of less than fifty yards six solid lines of gray were coming with their hats down, their bayonets at a charge, and the old familiar Rebel yell. Our first volley did not check their advance, but as volley after volley from our Spencer rifles followed, with scarce a second's intermission, and regiment after regiment [of Wilder's brigade] came on left into line on our right and poured the same steady deadly fire into their fast-thinning ranks, they broke and fled.'

The tremendous firepower of the repeating rifle magnified the impression of the flank attack. In addition, some 200 of Sheridan's men rallied, fired a short-range volley and charged Manigault's brigade from the front. Manigault's men retired to their start-line, the 24th Alabama losing its colours to a soldier in the 51st Illinois. Having struck a good blow, Wilder's men returned to their horses.

Manigault met Hindman's reserve, Anderson's Mississippi Brigade, advancing in the wake of Deas' brigade and their arrival brought fresh momentum to the assault. Together they encountered the last formed brigade of Sheridan's division. When Sheridan marched two brigades toward Thomas, he left Laiboldt as a reserve to support Davis. When the Confederate penetration began, it was well placed to counter-attack, but it was mistakenly deployed in column of regiments. Heedlessly, the corps commander, McCook, ordered them in. Laiboldt had no choice but to obey, and so passed the word to 'advance with charge bayonet'. The brigade advanced through the fleeing front-line troops. Trying to wheel to face the enemy, it received 'a murderous fire' from Deas and Anderson and was routed. The last Union reserve on this sector of the field was gone.

Sheridan's division had proven its valour in the past, and would do so again during an amazing charge at Missionary Ridge. Here at Chickamauga it was poorly served by its corps and army commanders and suffered accordingly. Sheridan would report many men shot down before they could even face the front. A remnant would contribute to the Federal rearguard, but that was all. The division was out of the battle, most of the men fleeing to the rear and leaving many to be taken prisoner.

Hindman's charge, one of the most successful infantry assaults of the war, had gained about a mile and a quarter but had outstripped the adjacent divisions and caused a gap to open between his and Johnson's command. In the resultant confusion the 15th Alabama, one of

Hood's units, fired into Hindman's rear. Pausing to sort out the confusion and reorganize his units, Hindman looked about, and much like Johnson, perceived that he was alone. Indeed there were no friendly troops within about a half-mile of his position. Then regiments on his left and rear reported smallarms and artillery fire pouring in against their open flank – this from Wilder's Lightning Brigade – while to his right and rear Hindman himself heard hot firing intensifying. He resolved to countermarch toward the firing on his right. During this march he encountered Bushrod Johnson.

Meanwhile, some twenty minutes into Longstreet's assault, the battle came to Old Rosy. He was observing two brigades of Van Cleve's division flank marching towards Thomas. The column had just halted for no apparent reason when an aide pointed towards Brannon's line saying, 'our men are giving way yonder'. The army commander replied that that was impossible, there were ample units defending the sector. Then, to his astonishment Rosecrans saw it was all too true. Van Cleve's brigades, marching in double column, were directly behind Brannon's position when fleeing troops came pouring through their formation. Shaken, the lead brigade managed to continue to Thomas's position. Sam Beatty's brigade was less fortunate. Its men had just halted and lain down to avoid the fire beating the rear of Brannon's position when caissons crashed through the ranks at great speed crushing several soldiers. Before there was time to recover, charging Confederates hit the disordered brigade and routed it.

So Rosecrans watched 'a perfect stampede – guns, caissons, fragments of regiments all . . . in one disordered mass'. McCook arrived to report that he had just ordered Laiboldt's brigade to confront the enemy and that he expected its advance to 'set matters right'. Then the Confederate masses emerged into the Dyer field and the full dimensions of his army's débâcle hit the commanding general. Charles Dana, the Assistant Secretary of War, happened to be present. He saw Rosecrans cross himself. 'Hello!' he thought. 'If the general is crossing himself, we are in a desperate situation.' Rosecrans was no coward. He had proven himself on many fields, but the sight

▲The view from Rosecrans' headquarters looking towards the Confederate breakthrough.

◄Kentucky-born, West Point graduate John Bell Hood enjoyed a meteoric rise by distinguishing himself on dozens of fields as regimental, brigade and division commander in the Army of Northern Virginia. Tall, thin and wiry, he had a grave face that belied his youth. He served in Longstreet's corps where his division earned the reputation as the hardest-hitting of a very tough lot. He suffered a severe arm wound at Gettysburg, but could not resist re-joining his men as they travelled west to Chickamauga. Aged 32, he commanded a corps under Bragg before being disabled by a grievous wound during his rupture of the Union right on the battle's second day. (Library of Congress)

of Longstreet's assault brigades sweeping forward broke his nerve. He turned to his staff and said, 'If you care to live any longer, get away from here.' To Dana's amazement, the headquarters of the Army of the Cumberland 'disappeared'.

The Union line no longer existed. Officers from Major General McCook down desperately tried to rally the men. Amid whistling Minié balls and exploding shells, McCook seized a flag and tried to get his men to stand. But the scare was on them and they would not. One of Rosecrans' staff relates that: 'All became confusion. No order could be heard above the tempest of battle. With a wild yell the Confederates swept on ... They seemed everywhere victorious.' Rosecrans was borne back in the retreat amid 'fugitives, wounded, caissons, escort, ambulances, [which] thronged the narrow pathways' leading to the rear. So desperate did the scene appear that Rosecrans concluded that the day was lost. When an officer appeared to ask for reinforcents for the Union forces still fighting around the Dyer field, he had to shout above the din of firing and the yell of the advancing Rebels in order to be heard. Rosecrans replied, 'It is too late, I cannot help.' Similarly, a badly shaken Major General Crittenden told his staff, 'I believe I have done all I can' and asked for suggestions. His chief of staff replied that he should go to Chattanooga to rally the town for defence and so Crittenden too left the battle. Such were the dimensions of the rout that Rosecrans, two corps, and four divisional commanders on this sector independently came to the same conclusion and abandoned the field. Thus they were not present to see what transpired in and around the Dyer field.

While Johnson and Hindman were achieving splendid results with their western Rebels, the men from the Army of Northern Virginia experienced a considerably tougher time. The three brigades of Hood's old division were among the Confederacy's élite shock troops. Just before the assault began Longstreet formed them in brigade column with a 100-yard separation between brigades. Led by Law's Alabama soldiers, the entire column moved forward at about the same time that Bushrod Johnson went in. After crossing the Lafayette Road Law's brigade received heavy enfilade fire on its right from elements of Brannon's division but very little from directly ahead. It continued to advance into this void until reaching the Dyer field where it became embroiled in a hot fire fight. Here Longstreet's insistence upon concentrated mass paid dividends. A soldier in the 44th Alabama stated that, 'Our lines were unusually short, and, as soon as one line was out of ammunition, another was rushed forward.'

Meanwhile, the second brigade, Georgians commanded by 'Rock' Benning, drifted to the right and were fighting against Brannon. The third brigade, Hood's famed Texas outfit, bypassed this uproar and continued towards the Dyer field, arriving in time to see McNair's and Gregg's gallant assault against Mendenhall's artillery po-

This Cavalry Sergeant Major carries a copy of the Enfield carbine and a Southern-made copy of the US cavalry sabre. Nathan Bedford Forrest, Bragg's cavalry commander, was particularly incensed by his superior's inactivity after Chickamauga. (Shirley Mallinson)

sition. The brigade commander, Brigadier General Jerome Robertson, changed front to his right and charged through the field. At first the Texans were facing mere stragglers and demoralized men, but on plunging into the woods the Texas brigade suddenly received a suprise close-range volley followed by a howling counter-charge that seemed to envelope both flanks. Robertson's men recoiled from contact, crying that they were 'flanked'.

The Yankees who performed this feat – seldom had the Texans recoiled from any enemy

– belonged to the 125th Ohio Volunteers commanded by Colonel Emerson Opdycke. The 125th was an untested unit, having joined Harker's brigade in Wood's division after the Battle of Murfreesboro, or Stones River as they preferred to call it. Pulled out of line when Wood rushed to assist Reynolds, elements of Harker's brigade escaped the lethal flank attack that hit units behind it. Although under severe fire, Opdycke executed a 180-degree change of front and began a rifle duel with Hood's men. Then General Wood

◀ *Freemantle saw Hood's men marching toward Gettysburg: 'They certainly are a queer lot to look at. They carry less than any other troops; many of them have only got an old piece of carpet or rug as baggage . . . all are ragged and dirty, but full of good humor and confidence in themselves and in their general, Hood.' (National Archives)*

▶ *Like their general, seen here, many of Hood's men were hit. A Texan described his experiences during the two days: 'When their line was broken . . . one fellow took a fair shot at me in an open place about thirty steps off. The bullet hit the handle of my bayonet . . . with great force, blinding and sickening me so that I fell . . . It seems to me that a thousand bullets and grapeshot tore up the ground around me.' He crawled to the rear and spent the night at a field hospital. 'Pretty sore but able to march', he rejoined*

his unit to receive '. . . a lick from something, I do not know what, on the wrist, which was very painful for a day or two, but when we found that the Yankees were gone and the field was ours, I was much rejoiced.' (Tennessee State Library)

ordered Opdycke to charge which the colonel thought a desperate thing to do. Hood's line seemed to be overlapping his own, but the regiment fixed bayonets and charged at the double.

To the Texans receiving the charge things appeared quite different. They believed themselves outnumbered and broke to the rear. Their tattered banners bore witness to the fact that they had spearheaded many desperate charges, including yesterday's when they had fought hard and well. On this field they simply made the veteran decision that it was someone else's turn. The colonel of the 3rd Arkansas spoke for them all when he described his men's fatigue as they went forward, how their lines became confused and ragged, and how, while reforming, they happily let two fresh brigades from McLaw's old division pass through their lines and thus 'the necessity of our returning to the fight was obviated'.

Not only was the Texas brigade mauled in the fight along the Dyer field, but Benning's Georgia brigade was wiped out to a man. At least this is what the excitable 'Old Rock' Benning believed. His brigade suffered frightfully in the fight against Brannon, seeming to melt away even while Benning watched. A bullet took down Benning's horse. Cutting a horse loose from a captured gun, using a rope as a riding whip, he remounted and galloped towards Longstreet to report. First he encountered a straggler and asked him where he was going. The Texan showed him his wound and Benning exclaimed, 'Great God! Is everybody killed? I have lost my brigade.' Hatless and nearly bursting, Benning found Longstreet just to the rear of Hood's column and said, 'General, I am ruined; my brigade was suddenly attacked and every man killed; not one is to be found. Please give orders where I can do some fighting.' Longstreet realized that the shock of combat had temporarily unnerved him, so he replied, 'Nonsense, General, you are not so badly hurt. Look about you. I know you will find at least one man, and with him on his feet report your brigade to me, and you two shall have a place in the fighting line.' Benning took the hint and returned to his command to rally his shattered brigade. Braced by his commander, Benning brightened even more when he saw the brigades of Kershaw and Humphreys pushing through the brush at the quick step.

Longstreet had delayed his assault until these units were in supporting positions and now his careful preparations paid off. But as the fight passed to Kershaw and Humphreys, Longstreet received the bad news that Federal cavalry, Wilder's men, were threatening his left flank. Although he ordered a brigade from Preston's reserve to help Hindman secure his open left flank, Longstreet largely brushed aside his subordinate's fears. He believed that the battle hinged along the heights behind the Dyer field and it was towards this point that he began massing his forces. He ordered Hindman to close to his right and link up with Johnson. Riding to Kershaw, aware that Opdyke's counter-attack had caused turmoil, he told the South Carolinian to mind his right flank so as to avoid further surprises. Then came a second piece of bad news. In the midst of the grand mêlée around the Dyer field, Hood had paid the price for his front-line leadership. He had been shot from the saddle and would lose a leg from this wound.

A noon recapitulation of the status of the Union forces lying in the path of the assault indicates the stunning impact of Longstreet's attack: two of Davis' and three of Sheridan's brigades fleeing towards a pass on Missionary Ridge; elements of two of Wood's brigades, two of Brannon's and elements of Negley's and Van Cleve's divisions fleeing towards McFarland Gap. With organized Federal opposition from the front all but ceased, Johnson, Hindman and Kershaw re-aligned their units at right angles to their original line of advance and faced north towards Thomas, north towards Chattanooga and north towards victory.

Exploitation

Having routed one-third of the Army of the Cumberland, a larger task awaited Longstreet's wing. It required a 90-degree wheel to the north, a difficult enough manoeuvre for such a large number of men when on the parade ground, a delicate, complex operation for troops under fire. Yankee artillery, firing from a spur of Missionary

Ridge, dominated much of the ground. At this time, shortly after noon, there were two hard knots of Federal resistance facing south towards Longstreet's breakthrough. One quite literally hinged on the remnant of Brannon's line. The other was the former artillery position – abandoned by Bushrod Johnson and reoccupied by a remnant of various Union commands – overlooking the Dyer field. While Humphreys tackled Brannon, Kershaw advanced through the Dyer field. Thus, it became a race to see if Brannon and like-minded officers could cobble together a new line facing Longstreet before Longstreet could re-orient his assault column to hit the vulnerable Yankee right flank.

When the Rebel breakthrough occurred, many of Davis' men fled through the rear of Brannon's adjacent division and crashed into one of Van Cleve's brigades and carried it to the rear. Brannon pulled his own rightmost brigade back in an effort to form a new line perpendicular to his original position. So rapid was the Confederate penetration that those regiments nearest the breakthrough were hit and routed before completing the change of front. Individual units fought well. The 82nd Indiana counter-attacked through the fleeing ranks of a sister regiment and managed to check Hood's on-rushing Rebels just as they came over the breastworks. When Humphreys' men joined the action the Confederate flood overlapped their flank and the 82nd broke and fled to the rear. Most of Brannon's two brigades adjacent to the breakthrough retired. 'The line being now broken', as Brannon later reported, 'and severely pressed at this point, and great confusion prevailing in the supports, composed of Wood's and Van Cleve's divisions, I formed the remnant of my command (and such stragglers from other commands as I could rally and bring into position) in line to resist, if possible, the pressure of the now advancing Rebels.'

Meanwhile Kershaw had reached the Dyer field and ordered the 3rd South Carolina to change front forward on his first company with the rest of the regiment conforming. The remainder of the command formed on the 3rd South Carolina and were thereby oriented towards the Federal position on the far side of the Dyer field, some 800 yards away. The Rebels advanced 200 yards, crossed a fence, and then Kershaw ordered them to fix bayonets and charge at the double. Moving through the corn and stubble field, they suffered considerably from artillery fire. To Colonel Opdycke, 'the whole line seemed perfect and as if moved by a single mind'. Kershaw's 'brave Palmetto boys' had got to within 100 yards of the enemy when the Yankees broke and ran.

After driving the shaken defenders from the fence line, the 3rd South Carolina penetrated another 100 yards into the woods before pausing for supports to arrive. The men from the Army of Northern Virginia now confronted a defensive position blessed by natural advantages and held by soldiers determined to sell their lives dearly. Kershaw did not immediately appreciate this. Believing that he was still pursuing a defeated foe, he urged regiments from a variety of commands – the Confederate brigades had become quite intermingled – to charge again. The fate of the 3rd South Carolina was the fate of all the charging units. It was brought up short by a terrible volley, and a murderous fire fight at 50 yards' range ensued. The situation worsened when Humphreys' brigade moved off at an angle leaving a gap on the Carolinians' right flank. The Yankees skilfully took advantage to pour enfilade fire into the regiment's flank, forcing it to withdraw to the shelter of a small ridge. Soon the entire South Carolina brigade recoiled. A soldier in the 2nd South Carolina said of the fighting to the top of one of the hills on Horseshoe Ridge, that without supports, 'it was too hot to stay there long'.

Bushrod Johnson told Longstreet that the Federal position on a dominant spur of Missionary Ridge was the 'key' to the battle. Longstreet agreed, 'It was the key, but a rough one.' With the Confederate dash through the Union right ended, and the first efforts to drive the Yankees from the spur of Missionary Ridge repulsed, a lull fell over the field. At 1 p.m. Longstreet scouted his northward-facing line only to be driven back by sharpshooters firing from behind trees and beneath bushes. It was thick, tangled ground and Longstreet could see little of the Federal line. Only the exchange of fire between rival skirmish lines marked the positions. Still, Lee's Old War Horse saw enough to realize that another major effort was required to achieve victory. Accordingly he rode back to Bragg's headquarters to try to coordinate a conclusive assault.

Longstreet found Bragg curiously disembodied from the desperate fighting that had taken place. Longstreet described his successful assault and explained the rationale for changing Bragg's

▶ *Longstreet met Bragg here, a headquarters deep in the woods and psychologically isolated from the battle. Years later Longstreet wrote with great understatement, 'From accounts of [Bragg's] former operations I was prepared for halting work, but this [Bragg's non-involvement] when the battle was at its tide and in partial success, was a little surprising.'*

plan. Although Bragg exhibited obvious displeasure that his plan had been altered, Longstreet continued by suggesting that Polk contribute troops to Longstreet's wing and then he, Longstreet, would lead them through a gap in Missionary Ridge, turn north and occupy the gap to Thomas's rear. Had this bold plan been attempted it might have destroyed Thomas's command, but Bragg was not equal to the opportunity. He had seen his own plan fail and did not seem interested in trying anyone else's. Many years later Longstreet claimed that Bragg believed the battle lost at this point. What is certain is that Bragg told Longstreet that nothing could be counted on from Polk's wing; they had done all they could, there were no other available reserves and he was retiring to his headquarters in the rear. Shocked by this behaviour, Longstreet returned to the front and tried to improvise an assault using his own resources.

As Longstreet's wing wheeled north toward Thomas, Rosecrans and those of his staff who could keep up, rode through a gap on Missionary Ridge and left the noise of battle behind. Reaching a fork in the road – one branch led north-west to Chattanooga, the other east through Rossville Gap and then south to Thomas – they paused to consider what to do next. Rosecrans wanted to rejoin Thomas while Chief of Staff Garfield went to Chattanooga to rally the fugitives, prepare the town for defence and organize supplies for the army. Overcome by the responsibility Garfield argued, 'I can go to General Thomas and report the situation to you much better than I can give these orders.' Rosecrans reluctantly agreed, telling Garfield to inform Thomas about efforts to form a rearguard and to give Thomas the latitude to continue the fight or to retreat. Then Rosecrans rode to Chattanooga, arriving at about 3.30 p.m. so exhausted in body and spirit that he required assistance to dismount. To an observer he had 'the terrible look of the brave man, stunned by sudden calamity'. In the words of historian Stanley Horn, 'Thus was presented the strange spectacle of a major conflict fought to its decisive close, one commander having fled the field, and the other sulking in his tent.'

The Rock of Chickamauga

At 2 p.m. the lull during which the Confederate line was re-oriented ended. Thomas's original line remained largely intact with divisions still manning the breastworks from where they had repulsed

◀ Confederates struggling up Horseshoe Ridge. One attacker, who was one of the only two men in his company to be unscathed, reported that his clothes were 'actually shot off me, like I had been picked'. (Tennessee State Library)

Polk during the morning. The tangled terrain in Thomas's right rear was the key ground. Here the Union line bent back at right angles to the line of breastworks and here the remnant of many Union divisions tried to hold the high ground on a spur of Missionary Ridge. Called Horseshoe Ridge, this crescent-shaped spur encompassed three separate hills as it descended from Missionary Ridge towards the Lafayette Road. The easternmost hill was 50 feet higher than the bare plateau on which the Snodgrass farm was situated. Longstreet's men faced the southern slope of Horseshoe Ridge. To capture it from this direction, the Rebels had to climb a heavily wooded, boulder-studded slope laced with deep ravines. The sun would set at six o'clock, twilight would last for a further eighty-four minutes. Since Civil War generals seldom attempted nocturnal assaults, this gave the Confederates about four and a half hours to take Horseshoe Ridge.

Already manning the line facing Longstreet were scattered fragments who had rallied around a handful of exceptional leaders such as Colonel Morton Hunter of the 82nd Indiana. Under Hunter's leadership the 82nd had already shown its valour during Brannon's initial desperate attempt to hold the Rebel breakthrough. After being swamped by overwhelming numbers and swept to the rear, Hunter began to rally his men. Retiring to the slopes of Horseshoe Ridge, he declared, 'I will not retreat another inch.' Some 350 men of Brannon's division joined him to face the next Rebel attack. So it was all along the ridge, individuals and squads – 40 men of the 44th Indiana with their colonel and their colours, 50 from the 31st Ohio led by a captain, handfuls of leaderless stragglers from a variety of commands – simply would not run. Officers who had no men to command picked up rifles and joined the defence. A senior sergeant told a handful of men from the 19th Ohio that they should retreat to rejoin their regiment. The men refused, saying '. . . we have the flag, some men from each company' and therefore '. . . "we are the regiment and will stay right here as long as we have ammunition" '. This hodgepodge of units, about 1,500 men, fought to buy time for Thomas to cobble together a defence of his right rear.

Not all were valorous. A key unit upon whom Thomas depended was Sirwell's brigade in Negley's division. Sirwell's was in support of its sister brigades holding Thomas's left when firing broke out back along Horseshoe Ridge. Responding to a plea for help from Brannon, Negley sent Sirwell's 21st and 74th Ohio. Sirwell himself conducted the 74th Ohio to its new position and then returned to his brigade only to find it gone. His divisional commander had marched it from the field! An Ohio private recalls marching into position on Horseshoe Ridge and fully expecting to find a strong line posted on this crucial ground. Instead, he was 'surprised that there were scarcely any troops in sight'.

Negley departed, grabbing the 74th Ohio in his haste to withdraw, leaving only one regiment from Sirwell's brigade. This regiment, the crack 21st Ohio, compensated for the others' absence. Taking up a position overlooking a deep ravine, armed with Colt revolving rifles, the 539-man regiment shot apart repeated attacks. But their rapid firing soon consumed their ammunition, and as Negley had taken the trains to the rear, there was no chance of resupply. The men searched the dead and wounded for ammunition and managed to hold firm throughout the long afternoon, repulsing a final charge that lapped to within 20 yards of its line.

During the early afternoon Thomas struggled to hold on to Horseshoe Ridge. A soldier recalls the scene: 'Immediately to our right sat on a large bay horse a general officer. He was utterly alone. The thunder of battle swept along the front . . . everywhere lines were wavering and crumbling like ropes of sand. But amid it all he was unmoved. A colonel rode up to him to ask, "How goes the battle?" "Very well, very well, sir! Move your line forward!" '

At about 3 p.m. Rosecrans' chief of staff arrived with news of the disaster on the Union right. Garfield found Thomas dealing with multiple crises. The Union-loyal Virginian calmly apprised Garfield of the situation, saying, 'We have repulsed every attack so far and can hold our ground if the enemy can be kept from our rear.'

By now Hindman and B. R. Johnson had completed their re-alignment against Horseshoe Ridge. Manigault's brigade spearheaded the

◀A West Point graduate and Mexican War veteran, 41-year-old Gordon Granger led the division-sized Reserve Corps during the Chickamauga campaign. His march to the sound of the guns (seen here) proved crucial in saving Thomas, and he became one of the heroes of the day. (US Army Military History Institute)

charge, losing 300 men in less than three minutes. Repulsed, they tried again. Slowly the attackers climbed the hotly contested slope. Their repeated assaults gradually decimated the defenders' ranks and numbed the survivors: 'The shoutings and commands of officers, the screams of shot and shell, the cries of the wounded, and the groans of dying men; the yells and cheering of friend and foe were all blended in one noise. While we were thus hanging between hope and fear ... a cry was raised, "Help is coming! Granger's Corps is coming!" '

The last orders Major General Gordon Granger, commander of the Reserve Corps, received on the night of the 19th came from Thomas and instructed him to post his command so as to be able to support the Union right. The next morning Granger watched the fight develop along Thomas's front with mounting anxiety. Although warned by his chief of staff that acting without orders might cost him his general's stars, Granger replied 'Don't you see Bragg is piling his whole army on Thomas? I am going to his assistance.' Granger's initiative saved the Union army.

Granger's van brigades, some 3,900 men commanded by Brigadier General Steedman, reached Snodgrass Hill just as Hindman's and Johnson's men gained the heights in Thomas's rear and began setting up a battery to enfilade the Union line. Thomas asked if Granger could retake the position. Granger replied, 'Yes ... They are raw troops and they don't know any better than to

charge up there.' Even as Thomas sent them in the battery opened up and canister flailed the ground about the two generals. As Granger's infantry were advancing up the slope the Rebel line suddenly rose from the ground 40 yards in front of them and delivered a terrible volley. Six officers leading one Ohio regiment fell in rapid succession. In contrast, the second in command of the 40th Ohio found his colonel trying to hide behind a tree 100 yards behind his line.

In the most conspicuous display of personal courage exhibited by any Union general, Steedman spurred up to the wavering 115th Illinois and ordered it to halt. Its colonel refused to lead it back up the slope, so Steedman sent him to the rear, seized the flag, and led the regiment himself. When his horse was killed he mounted another and continued to lead from the front. Steedman's men recaptured the heights. Still using Van Derveer's units as a fire brigade, Thomas added them to the defenders atop Horseshoe Ridge. A total of about 5,000 Yankees were now defending the ridge.

By 4 p.m. Longstreet's last reserve, two of Preston's brigades, had joined Kershaw's line facing Horseshoe Ridge. Hindman tried to work his way around the Union flank but made little progress. His men made repeated charges up the steep rocky terrain only to be repulsed by canister-firing Federal artillery at 40 yards' range. Hindman sent word to Kershaw that unless Kershaw could attract the enemy's attention, he would fail.

▶ *Harker's Brigade, employing regimental volleys, defends one of the three hills along Horseshoe Ridge. The 21st Ohio holds another crest until Hindman and B. R. Johnson launch a co-ordinated assault. The Confederates reach the top of the ridge, only to encounter Steedman leading Whitaker's brigade in a savage counter-attack.*

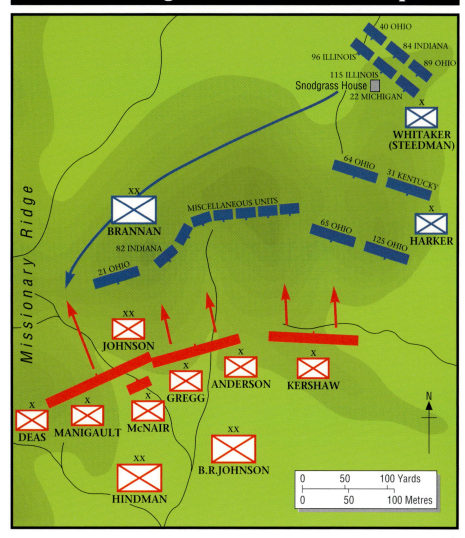

Horseshoe Ridge: situation about 2.30 p.m.

Accordingly Kershaw gathered all the forces he could, and using Preston's fresh men to spearhead the charge, tried again. The colour-bearer of the 7th South Carolina, Ensign Alfred Clark, took his customary place several paces in front of the line. The Carolinians advanced on the Yankee line – drawing so close that the defenders could plainly make out the small palmetto tree adorning the standard – and heard a Federal officer say in a loud voice that he would give a captain's commission to anyone who would capture the flag. Several defenders sprang forward, Clark was hit mortally and fell, but managed to throw the standard down the slope to his comrades.

By now most of the underbrush had been shot away. A defender described the scene: '. . . and we could see the gray legs of the front line . . . as they commenced the ascent . . . each [line] containing more men than in the thin, single line of defenders. "Don't waste any cartridges now, boys" was the only instruction given, as our line commenced firing – and the men in gray commenced falling; but they seemed to bow their heads to the storm of bullets, and picking their way among and over their fallen comrades . . . they came bravely and steadily on . . . the firing in their faces grew hotter . . . as the vacancies rapidly increased, they began to hesitate – "Now we've got 'em, see 'em wobble"

◄The defenders fought with great conviction. A veteran recalled: 'Every man seemed to know that here was the key to the position. This hill, taken by the enemy and Thomas's whole force, was either routed or captured. Word would pass along the line, "The Rebels are coming again! Don't leave this ground." ' (Tennessee State Library)

were the first words that passed in our line . . . then they halted and commenced firing wildly . . . turned and rushed madly down the slope, carrying the second line with them.'

Rosecrans had sent Thomas discretionary orders regarding a retreat, and by 4.30 Thomas could sense the build-up of irresistible Confederate pressure. His line was now bent into a compressed 'U' shape. He sent the divisions defending his original breastwork line an alert order preparatory to a retreat just as renewed Confederate attacks began to hammer his position. The distance between the extreme right and left of the Confederate army was about half a mile, but as a Confederate general later explained, '. . . neither wing nor any of the generals knew the relative position of the two extremes . . . Otherwise advantage might have been taken of it, [and] the gap closed.' Indeed, so poor was Confederate staff work that Longstreet knew nothing of Granger's march (although Forrest's cavalry had observed it from start to finish) until the Reserve Corps's counter-attack exploded in his face.

From Thomas's left came an assault that marked Polk's effort to assist Longstreet. Fittingly his nephew's brigade spearheaded the effort. Following its repulse in the morning, Lucius Polk had withdrawn his brigade to reorganize, replenish cartridge boxes and count noses. The morning's fight had cost the brigade some 350 killed and wounded. In late afternoon the brigade moved to

its right, deployed and, together with Cheatham's division, rushed forward. It struck the position defended by King's regulars. As before, a terrible volley of grape, canister and rifle fire flayed the line causing it to fall back to the top of a rise. With his men in danger of being routed, Polk ordered an attached Arkansas battery forward to give support. The battery commander replied that his horses 'could not live a moment under such a fire'. Polk ordered him to have the guns manhandled forward. Assisted by infantry volunteers, the Arkansas battery reached a small elevated plateau less than 200 yards from King's line and poured double-shotted canister into the regulars – a captured Union officer reported that just two shots killed and wounded 38 men in one company – which silenced the defenders' fire. Polk ordered a charge and his men responded eagerly, overrunning the works and capturing some 200 regulars.

Polk's assault coincided with Thomas's decision to retreat. He had hoped to hold on until nightfall, but at about 5 p.m. he realized that this would not be possible and sent orders to his divisional commanders to withdraw, beginning with Reynolds whom he intended should provide the rearguard. As Reynolds began to pull out the opposing Rebels received an order from Longstreet to charge. Reynolds withdrew towards the narrowing escape gap behind Snodgrass Hill. When Thomas rode to meet the retreating column, a pair of Union soldiers intercepted him to report alarming news. They had been looking for water in the ravine below Snodgrass Hill and had seen formidable masses of Confederate troops beginning to advance. Thomas reacted immediately, ordering Reynolds to change front to face the threat and charge. Switching seamlessly from march column to battle line, Turchin's brigade 'yelled, rushed forward, and broke to pieces the confronting columns of the Rebels. They fled pell-mell' losing 250 prisoners.

Turchin's charge temporarily secured the Federal line of retreat from pressure from the south. Next out of the salient came Palmer's division, followed by Johnson's. King's regulars saw these units retreating across their rear at the same time as Polk attacked from the front. All along the breastworks the opposing Confederates discovered the retreat and eagerly advanced up to and over the abandoned works. As the Rebels converged, pressure against the remaining defenders increased and renewed assaults, including Polk's successful penetration, against both of Thomas's flanks began. The Yankees had to traverse an ever-narrowing corridor that was swept by fire from three directions so the final Union retreat was not pretty. August Willich, who, together with Van Derveer, had acted as Thomas's fire brigade throughout the day, continued to fight a solid rearguard action. Willich watched the brigades withdraw from the salient. As the retreating regiments passed his position they cheered his men, but Willich reported that this did little to encourage them, but only reminded them that they were alone. 'Then the storm broke loose; first in small squads, then in an unbroken stream, the defenders rushed without organization over the open field, partly over and through my brigade.' The Confederates advanced batteries to spray the retreating Yankees with canister, but they did not challenge Willich's brigade, which continued to present a bold front. Willich withdrew up Snodgrass Hill and covered the army's retreat.

Inevitably some units did not get the word until too late. The colonel of one typical regiment reported that when a courier arrived with the the retreat order, he could not hear it over the roar of artillery and musketry. Then, when he saw adja-

cent regiments withdrawing, the colonel tried on his own initiative to order his men to fall back, only to be foiled when his shouting could not be heard over the noise. Sectors of his line retired while others continued to fight obstinately to hold their ground. In this manner many regiments lost their organization and began to break up, losing handfuls of men captured as the remainder stumbled through the forest to the rear. The commander of a regular battalion described the retreat: 'Over a wide corn-field, under a terrific fire of musketry, canister, and spherical case shot, my men steadily and slowly followed their color.' When the regulars reached the woods to the rear they faced about and fired a last defiant volley before leaving the field. Baird reported, 'My loss, up to the time of falling back, was small . . . In retiring it was great.'

The hard-fighting 21st Ohio was forgotten in the retreat. Standing alone at the far right rear, reduced to one round per man for its fast-firing Colt rifles, the 21st Ohio suddenly saw shadowy figures advancing. A soldier went forward to investigate but was captured by Mississippians of Trigg's brigade before he could alert his unit. This allowed Trigg's men to advance up the slope and open fire at close range. The 21st tried to run, only to encounter the 6th Florida looming in their rear. Some escaped, while others, surrounded and trapped, removed the chambers from the Colt's rifles to render them useless and surrendered. The regiment had 116 men taken prisoner here, giving it a cumulative loss of 265 out of the 500 men with whom it had begun the day.

All was confusion in the near darkness. The Confederate General Gregg rode up to a line of men to identify them, learned that they were the 35th Ohio, and 'received a volley . . . which riddled him and his horse'. The final collapse of the Federal line 'happened so quickly,' recalled one defender, 'that I had no time to run, but swung to the side of the tree . . . and looked into the muzzles of 50 or 60 Rebel guns pointing over the works'.

The two wings of Bragg's army met at last on the crest of Snodgrass Hill and began 'the wildest Confederate cheers and yells for victory', a chorus that spread all along the lines. Longstreet later wrote, 'The Army of Tennessee knew how to enjoy its first grand victory.'

AFTERMATH

On the night of the 20th Bragg believed his army crippled. He was not far from the truth. The battle had featured stand-up combat fought with uniquely western determination on both sides, and the result had been a vast slaughter. At about midnight Bishop Polk went to Bragg to announce that the enemy was 'fleeing precipitately from the field'. Bragg was not so sure, and arose next morning expecting to find the two armies still in contact. He knew his men were weary from hard marching and battle. Typically they were also short of provisions because Bragg had sent the supply trains far to the rear before the battle began. Hundreds of his army's horses were dead, which much reduced mobility. The troops had consumed prodigious amounts of ammunition and needed to replenish. For these reasons, as Bragg later explained in his report, it was necessary to pause and refit before renewing the fight. He rode to his picket line where he learned, for the first time, that the enemy had conceded the field. Bragg ordered pickets all along his army's front to advance, but did not launch a pursuit.

He met Longstreet who proposed that since 'the hunt was up' there was little to fear from the the dispirited Yankees and much to be gained by rapid movement. Longstreet had been schooled in

▼ *While their generals delayed, the Rebel soldiers inspected the battlefield and saw, '. . . the forest trees splintered and torn by the plunging shot and shell . . . dismounted caissons and artillery wheels, dead horses, guns, cartridge boxes, bayonets . . . Trees and saplings, not larger than a man's body to a height of six or eight feet, contained from a dozen to as high as sixty rifle balls . . . But worst of all [were the] upturned faces and glaring eyes, torn and mangled bodies . . . at the Snodgrass place, there were acres covered with wounded and many dead.' Here the victorious soldiers 'peel' their fallen enemies. (Library of Congress)*

the aggressive tactics of the Army of Northern Virginia; he suggested that they cross the Tennessee River north of Chattanooga thereby severing Rosecrans' line of communications and forcing him to abandon Chattanooga itself. He also received a report from Forrest who, typically, was pursuing the foe relentlessly. Forrest had seen a long wagon train crossing the Tennessee River and hastily dictated a report to Bragg: 'I think they are evacuating as hard as they can go . . . I think we ought to press forward as rapidly as possible.' It was the moment for decisive action. Bragg could either operate against Rosecrans' line of communications or march on Chattanooga directly and

▶ *The Confederates claimed to have captured 51 field pieces, a figure supported in a gun by gun tabulation made by an Ordnance Department officer. Moreover, several Rebel battery commanders exchanged worn or obsolete pieces for superior Yankee ordnance while on the field. Union reports, on the other hand, acknowledged the loss of 36 field pieces, although their own statistics yield a figure of 39. Whatever the truth of it, the Army of Tennessee certainly captured more artillery pieces during the battle than any other Confederate force captured during a field engagement at any time during the war.*

▶ *Bedford Forrest had a meeting with Bragg to urge a pursuit. Afterwards Forrest's orderly asked if the army was to advance: 'Terrific profanity, then, "I have written to him. I have sent to him. I have given him information on the condition of the Federal Army." Another stream of profanity. "What does he fight battles for?" '*
(Tennessee State Library)

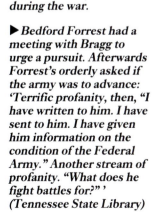

assault the city. Instead, he did neither, merely following his foe to Chattanooga, and passively investing the city.

Unlike Bragg, the soldiers had no doubts that an important victory had been won. A Florida gunner wrote on 21 September that 'we have whipped the Yankees badly'. A Tennessee soldier wrote, 'This is the only battle that I have ever fought in that we have held the battlefield, and it does me good to march across it, *northward*.' The Army of Tennessee had yet to fight a defensive battle, and its ferocious assaults had been costly, incurring at least 18,454 casualties. Stewart's division had suffered more than any other, two of

▼ *The Union army retreat to Chattanooga, seen in this period photograph with Lookout Mountain looming in the background. The day after the battle a Mississippi soldier wrote in his diary about a glorious victory, but added, 'Why the enemy have been allowed to get away so easily I am at a loss to know . . . There is something mysterious about this fight that remains to be solved.' (National Archives)*

▲ *Many survivors could only attribute their good fortune to divine intervention: 'My Dear Wife . . . I am just out of the titest place that ever I have bin in wee have had a very hard fight here on saterday and sunday I went through it un hurt dos seem that nothing but the finger of God could cary a man through such a seen.' (US Army Military History Institute)*

Confederate Regimental Losses at Chickamauga

	Engaged	Killed	Wounded	Missing	%
10th Tennessee	328	44	180	—	68.0
1st Alabama Btn	260	24	144	—	64.6
5th Georgia	317	27	165	2	61.1
2nd Tennessee	264	13	145	1	60.2
15/37th Tennessee	202	15	102	4	59.9
16th Alabama	414	25	218	—	58.6
6/9th Tennessee	335	26	168	—	57.9
18th Alabama	527	41	256	—	56.3
22nd Alabama	371	44	161	—	55.2
23rd Tennessee	181	8	77	13	54.1
29th Mississippi	368	38	156	—	52.7
58th Alabama	288	25	124	—	51.7
37th Georgia	391	19	168	7	50.1
63rd Tennessee	402	16	184	—	49.7
41st Alabama	325	27	120	11	48.6
32nd Tennessee	341	9	156	—	48.3
20th Tennessee	183	8	80	—	48.0
1st Arkansas	430	13	180	1	45.1
9th Kentucky	230	11	89	2	44.3

Of the top twenty reported percentage losses of all Confederate regiments in all battles, six occurred at Chickamauga

◀ *Bragg unleashed Wheeler's cavalry corps, seen here capturing a supply train, against Rosecrans' communications. The Army of the Cumberland endured short rations until Grant arrived to restore the situation. (Tennessee State Library)*

▼ *An Illinois soldier wrote to his mother that all he had to eat was one ear of corn for the day, 'But Old Rosey Rosecrans won't fall back nor I won't.' (US Army Military History Institute)*

▲ *On 4 October the Bragg-hating clique of high-ranking officers, including Simon Buckner (seen here), composed a circular letter to the Commander Jefferson Davis: 'Two weeks ago this army, elated by a great victory which promised to be the most fruitful of the war, was in readiness to pursue its defeated enemy. That enemy, driven in confusion from the field, was fleeing in disorder and panic-stricken across the Tennessee River. Today, after having been twelve days in line of battle in that enemy's front . . . the Army of Tennessee has seen a new Sebastopol rise steadily before its view.' (Tennessee State Library)*

its brigades being among the four that received the greatest battering. Clayton and Bate suffered 44 and 51 per cent losses, respectively. Gregg's brigade, which had operated adjacent to these units, also lost 44 per cent casualties. Heading the doleful list of valour was Benning's Georgia Brigade, which had come west to suffer a staggering 56.6 per cent loss. Officer losses had been particularly high. For example, four of the brigades in Walker's command took 33 field officers – captains up to colonels – into action and lost three killed, nineteen wounded and one missing.

The young men of both armies accepted death in an astonishingly matter of fact manner. An Alabama soldier saw his brother hit with 'a minnie ball in the left breast penetrating his left lung' as they were charging forward on the 20th. The soldier visited his brother the next day: 'He is very calm all the time and quite rational, talking freely about death . . . he did not expect to be killed in the war, desired to see his wife and children and die at home, did hope to raise his children, but is resigned to the will of God.' One of Hood's Texans echoed this sentiment: 'My Precious Wife: God has heard your prayers, and through His mercy I am preserved through the perils of another great battle, far more dangerous in its individual and personal incidents to our brigade than any of the war. The oldest soldiers agree that they have never seen the like.'

Across the lines, the Army of the Cumberland experienced, for the first time, the bitterness of defeat. A soldier in the 25th Illinois concluded, 'I guess we were better whipped than ever before.' An Ohio soldier said that the more his comrades looked at it, the more serious it seemed: 'Thus far in our service we had never retreated from any field of action, nor left our dead and wounded.' The battle had cost the army at least 16,170 men, and now they sat in Chattanooga gazing at the Rebels holding the heights above.

When Bragg failed to press his advantage, morale recovered. A Federal soldier wrote that the anticipated assault on the town had not yet come and, 'I expect their waiting so long has bin a good thing for us. They say we have got a big reinforcements clost at hand. If that is so we will send old Bragg back a howling.' Indeed, over the

▲ *In Grant's reorganization, Gordon Granger assumed command of a corps consolidated from the much battered XX and XXI corps. Crittenden, McCook and Negley (seen here) were all relieved of command. (Tennessee State Library)*

succeeding weeks, some 37,000 Union reinforcements came to the aid of the army besieged in Chattanooga. Moreover, alarmed at the persistent panic in Chattanooga – Lincoln said that Rosecrans reminded him of a duck who had been hit on the head – the president ordered the hero of Vicksburg to take over. He offered Grant the option of keeping Rosecrans, but Grant preferred Thomas. So Thomas, already being called 'the Rock of Chickamauga', rose to the top of the Army of the Cumberland.

Union Regimental Losses at Chickamauga

	Engaged	Killed	Wounded	Missing	%
51st Illinois	209	18	92	18	61.2
26th Ohio	362	27	140	45	58.5
96th Illinois	401	39	134	52	56.1
25th Illinois	337	10	171	24	54.9
14th Ohio	449	35	167	43	54.5
8th Kansas	406	30	165	25	54.1
35th Illinois	299	17	130	13	53.5
87th Indiana	380	40	142	8	50.0

The South could not match the Union build-up. D. H. Hill believed that the battle had been decisive: 'It seemed to me that the élan of the Southern soldier was never seen after Chickamauga.' Soldiers realized that Chickamauga represented a gamble, that by denuding other fronts to reinforce Bragg, 'what had to be done must be done quickly'. Instead, when Bragg failed to act, the gamble was lost. The Confederate soldier 'fought stoutly to the last,' concluded Hill, 'but, after Chickamauga, with the sullenness of despair and without the enthusiasm of hope. That "barren victory" sealed the fate of the Southern Confederacy.'

◀*Rosecrans became swept up in the rout of his right wing, a débâcle that led to his dismissal shortly afterwards. In later years acquaintances believed they could still see the ghosts of Chickamauga in his once confident eyes. (National Archives)*

THE BATTLEFIELD TODAY

Chickamauga was a complicated battle. It is best studied on the spot. The Federal government established the site as a national park in the 1890s. At that time veterans of the battle assisted in laying out the battle lines and monuments. Because of this, the park today is maintained in close to its historic condition. The Visitors' Center offers an audiovisual programme, a useful tour guide and a fine collection of weapons. The entrance is guarded by excellent representative examples of artillery types. Vistors can follow a seven-mile driving tour which hits the battle's highlights. Better still, walk the lines and follow some of the woodland paths that traverse the field. As with all battlefields, nothing substitutes for a foot tour in order to gain an appreciation of the terrain. Having made repeated visits, I can vouch for the fact Chickamauga offers surprises and rewards to the diligent student.

Nearby Chattanooga remains 'the gateway to the Confederacy'. From this base, a two-hour drive north takes one to Murfreesboro and the well-preserved park at Stones River. Chattanooga itself has grown greatly and has largely taken over Missionary Ridge, but it is still instructive to visit this site where the Army of the Cumberland gained its revenge for Chickamauga. Lookout Mountain offers both a scenic and historic climb. The enterprising tourist can then follow Sherman's army, and my great-grandfather's march to Atlanta.

▼ *The Army of the Cumberland spearheaded Grant's offensive. Many of the soldiers shouted 'Chickamauga!* *Chickamauga!' as they charged up Missionary Ridge. (Library of Congress)*

CHRONOLOGY

1860
November: Abraham Lincoln elected President.
December: South Carolina votes to secede.

1861
9 February: Jefferson Davis elected President of the Confederate States of America.
12 April: Southern artillery opens fire on Fort Sumter.

1862
6-7 April: Battle of Shiloh.
18 June: Buell begins first campaign against Chattanooga.
27 June: Bragg assumes command of Army of Tennessee.
28 August: Bragg marches from Chattanooga to invade Kentucky.
8 October: Surprise Confederate assault initiates Battle of Perryville. McCook's corps routed while Sheridan holds his ground.
18 October: Bragg decides to retreat; the invasion ends in failure.
30 October: Rosecrans relieves Buell as commander of Army of the Cumberland.
31 December: Surprise Confederate assault initiates Battle of Murfreesboro (Stones River).

1863
3-4 January: When Rosecrans refuses to retreat, Bragg withdraws his army from the field.
24-6 June: Rosecrans advances from Murfreesboro. Wilder's 'Lightning Brigade' captures Hoover's Gap, opening route around Bragg's flank.
30 June: Bragg withdraws over Tennessee River. In nine-day campaign, costing only 560 casualties, Rosecrans captures central Tennessee.
1-3 July: Battle of Gettysburg, high-water mark of Confederate 'eastern' strategy.

4 July: Vicksburg surrenders. Bragg withdraws to Chattanooga.
15 August: After securing line of communications, Rosecrans advances again.
4 September: Walker's division en route to Bragg from Mississippi.
9 September: Rosecrans occupies Chattanooga. Longstreet begins rail transfer west. Buckner joins Bragg.
10 September: Rosecrans scatters his army in pursuit. Bragg orders attack against Negley's isolated division.
11 September: Hindman's excessive caution foils Bragg's plan.
12 September: Rosecrans comprehends his danger and begins to concentrate army.
13 September: Polk's blunder foils Bragg's planned attack against another isolated Federal force.
17 September: Rosecrans' concentration partially complete, the rival armies face off across Chickamauga Creek. Bragg plans his attack.
18 September, a.m. Hood's three brigades arrive. Bragg's army closes on Chickamauga Creek.
18 September, p.m. Hood forces Reed's Bridge; Walker fails at Alexander's Bridge.
19-20 September: Battle of Chickamauga
19 September, a.m. Brannon and Baird attack Forrest and Walker.
19 September, p.m. Fighting escalates as battle line extends southwards; three CSA assaults rock Union line.
11 p.m. Bragg reorganizes army into two wings.
20 September, 5.30 a.m. Hill receives his attack orders.
9.30 a.m. Breckinridge attacks.
10 a.m. Gist supports Breckinridge; Cleburne attacks.
10.45 a.m. Rosecrans mistakenly learns that Brannon is 'out of line'.

10.55 a.m. Wood receives order to close on Reynolds.
11 a.m. Stewart attacks.
11.30 a.m. Balance of Longstreet's wing attacks.
12-1 p.m. Union right collapses; Thomas stands alone.
1 p.m. Longstreet reorientates his wing against Thomas.
2 p.m. Longstreet's wing begins piecemeal assaults against Horseshoe Ridge.
2.30 p.m. Steedman reinforces Thomas.
3.30 p.m. Rosecrans reaches Chattanooga.
4 p.m. Longstreet launches final effort.
4.30 p.m. Thomas prepares to retreat; Polk renews assault.
5-5.30 p.m. Thomas withdraws from field.
20 September: Bragg initiates dilatory pursuit.
21 September: Army of the Cumberland retreats into Chattanooga; Bragg invests city.
23 September: Lincoln decides to send two corps from Army of the Potomac to reinforce Rosecrans.
26 September: Anti-Bragg cabal meets to try to remove Bragg.
30 September: Wheeler begins raid against Rosecrans' communications.
31 September: Bragg relieves Polk, blaming him together with Hindman and Hill for failed campaign.
9 October: Jefferson Davis visits army and decides to keep Bragg in command.
17 October: Grant takes command of all forces west of the Alleghenies to the Mississippi; decides to relieve Rosecrans and replace him with Thomas.

23 October: Grant arrives in Chattanooga.
27 October: Grant launches successful manoeuvre to open up supply line to Chattanooga.
5 November: Bragg detaches Longstreet's corps to Knoxville, fatally weakening his own army.
23 November: Sherman's divisions from Vicksburg prepare to attack Bragg's right.
25 November: Grant's double envelopment falters. Army of the Cumberland storms Missionary Ridge and routs Bragg's army.
28 November: Bragg asks to be relieved of command.
16 December: Davis appoints Joseph Johnson to command Army of Tennessee.

1864
30 January: Rosecrans assumes backwater assignment as commander of Department of Missouri.
7 May: Sherman, commanding army group based on Chattanooga that includes Thomas's Army of the Cumberland, begins Atlanta campaign.
17 July: Hood replaces Johnson and begins bloody counter-offensive.
2 September: Atlanta falls, securing Lincoln's re-election.
30 November: Hood's invasion of Tennessee leads to Battle of Franklin where the Confederate army is slaughtered. Its losses include many general officers who had fought at Chickamauga.
9 December: Following election, Rosecrans shelved for good.
15-16 December: Thomas routs Hood at Battle of Nashville.

WARGAMING CHICKAMAUGA

The actual fighting covered an expansive area and involved large forces, and therefore big battle rules are needed to cope with the action. I would recommend the increasingly popular 'Fire and Fury' (1990) which are specifically aimed at refighting the big battles of the war and use the brigade as the smallest unit of tactical manoeuvre. Skirmishers and regimental level tactics are not catered for and ranges and movement are basic and easily internationalized which makes for a fast game. By using 15mm figures to the larger ground scale, i.e., 65 yards to the inch, it is possible to take in all the action on a 9ft × 6ft table. This takes in the action from the Cloud Church (used as a field hospital for the Union left) almost to Lee and Gordon's Mill.

With 6/10mm figures it is possible to use the smaller ground scale for 'Fire and Fury' of 45 yards to the half-inch and take in the distance from Crawfish Springs to Cloud Church. On a 9ft table this gives a battle front of 9,720 yards and on the large scale of 65 yards to the half-inch gives a battle front of 14,040 yards. The latter option makes it possible to represent Granger's Corps actually on table and allows for the use of cavalry guarding flanks and wagon trains.

Creating the Table Top Battlefield

The enjoyment and sense of 'being there' in any wargame does not so much depend on the professional appearance of the model soldiers in use but more on the presentation of the table-top scenery. Not only should the scenic effects be of reasonable quality, but they should be accurately placed on the table-top battlefield in order to create the correct conditions, for battlefield tactics were very much influenced by the terrain across which the armies fought.

Constructing the table-top battlefield for Chickamauga does not pose any great problems. The battlefield, apart from 'Horseshoe Ridge', was flat. The ridge is an important feature and must be represented. Because there is only this one area of high ground it may well be a good idea to model it specifically for the purpose of the refight using polystyrene set on a plywood base and covered with a filler–paper mash mixture, then painted. The hill should have gentle slopes to facilitate the positioning of model figures and a flat-topped area upon which the Snodgrass House can be positioned. Any log cabin building will suffice for this since the building is not in any way distinctive enough to warrant a special model, but contemporary sketches and photographs exist from which the building can be scratch built. The same is true of most other battlefield buildings, but Lee and Gordon's Mill may be considered worthy of a scratch-built project as might McAffee's Church. I am not sure if there are any illustrations of the church available, but there are several photographs showing different views of the white three-storey mill; the gable end facing away from the river bears the legend 'LEE & GORDON'S' and beneath this centrally 'MILLS' in traditional western-style lettering.

Before placing the trees on the table and after fixing the position of the high ground and buildings, the next stage is to mark out the roads. The important roads to mark in are the La Fayette, Ringold, Reed's Bridge, Alexander's Bridge, and Crawfish Springs roads. These routes were used by both sides in manoeuvring their divisions into place. Other tracks intersecting the woods need not be represented in such a grand tactical game as most brigades were deployed and made little use of marching columns in the actual battle area. Roads can be made up with strips of yellowish-brown card, but these are liable to shift around if not fastened down. For a much tidier appearance, I recommend masking tape which comes in an appropriate coulour but can be further enhanced with coloured pastels by those with an artistic bent. It is possible to purchase stretchy tape which can be used to mask off curved areas and this type is preferable though not essential as the roads followed a generally straight direction. Two-inch-wide blue masking tape, or mottled blue-and-white plasterer's masking tape which is more ideal can also be used to depict the Chickamauga River, or river sections can be made up or bought commercially. The edges of the river can be disguised with cork (for rocks) and lichen (for bushes).

Once the roads are in position place in the field areas. It is probably necessary to make these field areas to fit the configuration of the actual battle-field fields and these will have defined corners of near 90 degrees. Interesting fields can be made from textured materials, but beware of some textures as figures may not stand well on them. Clearings will have an irregular outline. Roads and fields should be fenced off. In 15mm, fences are quite easy to come by and in the case of the worm fences that proliferated, easy to construct from match wood or similar. In 6mm and 10mm, suitable fences are more difficult to come by and manufacture. I made my worm fences from piano wire set on lollypop sticks and cemented with plastic padding which is stronger than super-glue. Log breastworks are also required for the Union forces on the second day, and can be made from lengths of thin dowel mounted on a wooden base. These temporary log breastworks were movable and perhaps a move of quarter normal distance could be allowed for a brigade to transport its breastworks. Once behind breastworks it was difficult to get troops out to attack and perhaps a manoeuvre penalty needs to be imposed.

Much of the battlefield is wooded and there-fore a good supply of trees are required. If the American Civil War or Revolutionary War are your main wargaming interests, it is most desirable to have a good stock of model trees in any case since woodlands were common to many battlefields. The trees are then placed all over the remainder of the table. Do not forget that model troops have

to be moved through these woods so it is best to mount the trees individually or in clumps so that they can be moved around an area out of the way of the model figure bases The woods are con-sidered as open with some denser patches, espe-cially nearer the river. Visibility in woods is a maximum 150 scale yards.

Deploying the Wargames Forces for the First Day on the Grand Tactical Scale

If a big enough table is available, it is preferable to deploy all forces as the situation stood at dusk on the evening of the 18th. Each brigade should be represented by two markers – one the actual brigade and the other a dummy. Markers should be of a constant size, say 5in × 2in in blue for the Union and gray for the Confederates. Each marker should be marked underneath with the brigade commander's name or 'dummy' and revealed whenever two markers approach within 18 inches (9 inches if using 6/10mm figures) or if in woods within 6 inches (3 inches if using 6/10mm figures) of one another. Revealed dummy markers are removed from play. Actual brigades are only set on table if they are seen by an actual enemy unit. Such dispositions can be obtained from 'Battles & Leaders' Vol.III, p.648. It might well be possible for Thomas to throw back Bragg's movement across the Chickamauga or for D. H. Hill to roll up the Union right from Crawfish Springs. As noted above, 6/10mm figures are necessary to do this effectively, and a table-top scale size of 8 scale miles length is necessary. However there is no guarantee that the divisions will end up in their historical locations to begin the battle on the 19th. If such a set piece is required the actual battle front of the historical action can be focused in on it.

In order to come somewhere near to repre-senting the tactical situation as it stood on the morning of 19 September 1863, the forces of the respective sides should be set up as near as possible in the positions they occupied at 7.30 a.m., when Thomas' XIV Corps opened the battle against Walker's Corps supported by Forrest, west of Jay's Saw Mill between the Reed's bridge and Alexander's Bridge roads. The dispositions should be made randomly as there was a deal of intermixing of formations. Brannon of Thomas's corps held the right with Baird also of Thomas's on his right; then came Johnson's division of McCook's corps and then Palmer's division of Crittenden's corps extending the line to the south. From Palmer, Reynolds' division of Thomas, extended the line to south-westwards with Van Cleve of Crittenden coming up on Palmer's right across the La Fayette road. As the Union brigades marched northwards, the fighting drifted southwards and Brannon was brought in on Van Cleve's right along with Beatty's Brigade of Negley's division/ Thomas's corps coming up to the rear of the Dyer House. Davis's division of McCook, Wood's division of Crittenden then Sheridan's division of McCook prolonged the Union line southwards along the La Fayette State Road beyond the Viniard Farm. Wilder's 'Lightning' Brigade (armed with Spencer rifles and mounted on white horses) of Reynolds' division, were in reserve just south of the Widow Glenn's orchard, having just retired from delaying the Rebel movement across Alexander's Bridge and soon to be called on again to save the Union right flank. Negley's division of Thomas' corps was on Wilder's left in front of the Dyer farm and behind Davis and Wood.

On the Rebel side of the La Fayette Road, Cheatham's division was to the rear and coming up between Walker's left and Stewart's right, the latter with his division in column of brigades poised to assail Van Cleve in the Union Centre. Bushrod Johnson's division was marching up on Stewart's left with Law on his right ready to deliver a punch that would send the Yankees reeling back across the La Fayette Road. Marching northwards across Thedford's Ford then Alexander's Bridge was Cleburne who was coming up to deliver the final attack of the first day on the Union left.

On the south flank Lytle's brigade of Sheridan's division guards the bridge at Lee and Gordon's Mill as Breckinridge prepares to continue his march northwards from a position nearly a mile eastwards. Farther south again Wheeler's and Crook's cavalry keep vigil on their flanks. Some four miles from Thomas's position on the Ringold Bridge Road is Granger's Union Reserve Corps, its rear covered by McCook's cavalry.

The scene is set, the troops are deployed. Rosecrans is placed in his HQ at the Widow Glenn's house where he stayed throughout the battle – not even venturing out to check his dispositions following Kellogg's erroneous report of the gap in his lines – until it was overrun by Longstreet's charge on the second day. Bragg apparently used an ambulance as a mobile headquarters. His whereabouts proved problematical for his subordinates during the battle, but possibly Alexander's Bridge is a likely command post for the Confederate commander-in-chief.

Assessing the Quality of Commanders and Troops

Like many other battles, Chickamauga demonstrates how important were the commanders on the spot. The men who could inspire and lead their troops to victory were those who shared the dangers of the front line. Neither Bragg nor Rosecrans involved themselves in the battle and although Rosecrans had his headquarters very near the front his movements were lethargic. Perhaps the commanders need to be restricted in their ability to move, say a six must be thrown at any time either of the C-in-Cs wishes to move his personality figures. The same restrictions should also be applied to Lieutenant Generals D. H. Hill and Polk during the first six game turns of each day of battle. In the main however, Confederate commanders tended to lead their troops from the front in order to inspire confidence in the attack, but as a result tended to get injured regularly. The Confederate infantry, at least up to and including Chickamauga, were certainly more aggressive and willing to take the tactical offensive. The Union troops tended to rely on their artillery to break the élan of the Rebels and their main commanders, Rosecrans, Thomas, Crittenden and McCook, were cautious and should therefore inspire their troops only if they are fighting defensively. Granger and Steedman and Sheridan were rather more combative. Of the Union commanders, Thomas, Granger, Sheridan, Steedman, Van Derveer, Wilder and Willich would qualify as exceptional leaders. On the Confederate side Longstreet, Hood, Cleburne, Breckinridge, Stewart, Johnson,

Kershaw and Forrest would all rate as exceptional higher formation leaders with the best brigade commanders being those of Cleburne's, Breckinridge's, Hindman's, Liddle's, Stewart's and Johnson's divisions.

The ability of the brigade commanders have a direct bearing on the quality of their troops. Some brigades may be additionally considered as crack troops such as Armstrong's cavalry, Deshler's, McNair's infantry and those of Hood's Corps from the Army of Northern Virginia on the Confederate side and Wilder's brigade and possibly King's regulars on the Union side. While most of the troops on both sides were veterans of Perryville and Stones River there were some greenhorn units in both armies, i.e., Preston's division and many units of Hindman's division on the Confederate side and the whole of Granger's corps on the Union side.

Tactical Scenario Possibilities

Many big battles offer scope for sectioning off parts of the larger picture and exploring the tactical scene at a lower level. The regiment as the basic unit of manoeuvre has been long established in wargaming and many rules are designed for this level of game. Among ACW fans, 'Johnny Reb' (1988, Games Design Workshop) rules are perhaps the most widely used for combat up to corps level. In fact the scenario booklet that comes with the rules features two actions set in the Chattanooga Campaign period. The first of these concerns Wilder's brigade at Hoovers Gap on 16 July and Breckinridge versus Negley at dawn on 19 September before the forces marched north from Crawfish Springs and Glas Mill. There is also a scenario booklet available entitled *To the Sound of the Guns* (1988, GDW), which features Thomas's attack on Walker and Forrest. These scenarios point the way to the development of others.

During his advance from Chatanooga, Rosecrans boldly spread his army far and wide hoping to outflank Bragg and force his retreat as he had done at Chatanooga. Meanwhile Bragg was concentrating his at La Fayette and Thomas, in the belief that Bragg was in retreat, was heading straight towards it with his nearest support, Crittenden's corps, fifteen miles away. Fortunately, as Thomas's lead commander crossed McLermore's Cove, Negley realized that something was wrong and fell back to a wood facing north expecting an attack from Hindman's division. But Hindman would not attack. Baird came up to reinforce Negley. After two days, when Cleburne's division advanced, Thomas had withdrawn his divisions from Stevens' Gap. Had the Confederate commanders acted with alacrity a large part of Thomas's command could have been destroyed in McLermore's Cove. This has the makings of an excellent 'what might have been' scenario.

A small-scale scenario could involve Wilder's delaying action against Walker's attempt to cross Alexander's Bridge, with Forrest arriving to see off the Federals. Another delaying action might concern Forrest's efforts to prevent Granger from reinforcing Thomas, with McCook's cavalry holding off the Rebels. Another scenario could be teased out of the main battle this time, the assault on Horseshoe Ridge. Will Granger come as promptly to Thomas's assistance in the wargame and can the Confederates capture the hill by dusk? Such imponderables make for entertaining games. And entertainment is what wargaming should be about.

Refighting Chickamauga Without Figures

For many people board wargames are a convenient way into wargaming and the understanding of military history, and there are several versions of the battle available. The battle can also be played on computer with SSI's 'Rebel Charge at Chickamauga'. The version I have seen is for the Amstrad PC. The game recreates the battle in thirteen two-hour turns.

INDEX

(References to illustrations are shown in **bold**.)